THE KILLING OF
SISTER GEORGE

A Comedy by

FRANK MARCUS

SAMUEL FRENCH

LONDON

NEW YORK   TORONTO   SYDNEY   HOLLYWOOD

THE KILLING OF SISTER GEORGE

Produced by Michael Codron, in association with Bernard Delfont, at The Duke of York's Theatre, London, on the 17th June 1965, with the following cast of characters—

(in the order of their appearance)

JUNE BUCKRIDGE (Sister George)	*Beryl Reid*
ALICE 'CHILDIE' McNAUGHT	*Eileen Atkins*
MRS MERCY CROFT	*Lally Bowers*
MADAME XENIA	*Margaret Courtenay*

Directed by VAL MAY

Designed by CATHERINE BROWNE

SYNOPSIS OF SCENES

The action of the play passes in the living-room of a London West End flat

ACT I

A Tuesday afternoon in late September

ACT II

SCENE 1   A week later. 4 a.m.
SCENE 2   Late afternoon of the same day

INTERLUDE

ACT III

Two weeks later. Morning

Time—the present

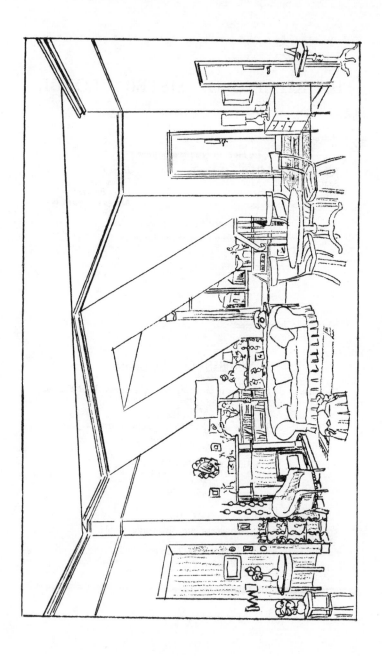

THE KILLING OF SISTER GEORGE

ACT I

SCENE—*The living-room of a London West End flat. A Tuesday afternoon in late September.*

Down R is a wide arch showing part of a small entrance hall which leads to the front door of the flat. The fireplace is R, above the arch, and is fitted with an electric fire. Up RC, facing the audience, under a sloping ceiling, is a window with a narrow window-seat, overlooking roofs. Up L is a low, wide rostrum, reached by two long steps, which forms a wide corridor leading off up L to the bathroom. In the back wall of the corridor, facing the audience, is the bedroom door. There is a banister rail along the right side of the rostrum. In the wall L is a serving hatch, which when open shows a glimpse of kitchen shelves. The door to the kitchen is down L, below the hatch. The furniture, an incongruous mixture of antique, nineteen-thirtyish and modern, looks expensive but ill-assorted. Down R is a small table with a single chair in front of it. On the wall over the table is a two-way speaker on an extending arm. Above the arch R there is a whatnot with Victorian china ornaments on its shelves. In front of the whatnot, facing L, is a small tub armchair. Above the fireplace is a long bookcase and there is a canterbury against the wall R of the window. A bureau-type radiogram is L of the window. A low coffee-table stands L of the bedroom door, on the rostrum. A long sideboard is underneath the serving hatch L and a small occasional table and an upright chair are down L, below the kitchen door. A sofa with a table behind it is RC. There is a telephone on the table. A circular, pedestal table is LC with chairs R and L of it. A pouffe is down RC. The hall is furnished with a small table and an umbrella vase. At night the room is lit by a standard lamp up R and table-lamps down R and L. There is a light switch below the fireplace.

Before the CURTAIN rises, as the house-lights fade, the 'Applehurst Theme', a cheerful folk-dance tune, is heard.

When the CURTAIN rises, the music fades. The room is empty. The front door is heard to slam off R. JUNE BUCKRIDGE enters from the hall. She is a rotund, middle-aged woman, wearing a belted white mackintosh. She carries a leather brief-case and string gloves. She is very agitated.

ALICE (*off in the kitchen; calling*) George? George, is that you?

(JUNE *shows exasperation at the sound of Alice's voice, throws her gloves and brief-case on to the sofa and goes to the table behind it. She opens a cigar box on the table, finds it empty and throws it violently on to the floor up C, then moves to the fireplace.* ALICE 'CHILDIE'

McNaught, *in the kitchen, opens the hatch and looks into the room. She is a girl-woman in her thirties, looking deceptively young. She conveys an impression of pallor: her hair, eyes and complexion are all very light. She is wearing a sweater and jeans, with a plastic apron and orange rubber gloves*)

(*Surprised*) George, what on earth . . .?

(June *takes a cheroot from a box on the mantelpiece, reaches for the lighter, finds a doll in long clothes in the way and throws it into the fender*)

George! What are you doing at home at this time of the afternoon?

(June *lights her cheroot and moves down* R *of the sofa*)

June (*after a pause*) They are going to murder me.
Alice. What . . .?
June (*moving* LC) I've suspected it for some time.
Alice. What . . .?
June. Kindly close that hatch. (*She moves to* R *of the table* LC *and removes her coat*)

(Alice *quickly closes the hatch and comes into the room by the kitchen door* L. *She carries a tea-cloth*)

Alice. George, I don't understand what you're saying—what are you talking about?

(June *puts her cheroot on the rim of the ashtray on the table* LC)

June (*brutally*) Shut up! You know nothing. (*She moves* RC, *below the sofa*)

(Alice, *silenced, watches* June's *nervous pacing*)

That Australian bitch, that Sheila, let it out.
Alice (*sitting* R *of the table* LC) The one who used to be a lady cricketer?
June (*with disgust*) Yes, that's her—the lolloping great trollop! (*She removes her coat*)
Alice. So, what did she say?
June (*very excited*) It was during the tea-break; she handed me my cup of tea and said, 'I trust you're in good health', she said with a sly wink.
Alice. There's nothing wrong with that.
June (*tossing her coat into the armchair* R) I knew what she meant. I got the message all right. (*She moves up* RC)
Alice (*rising, crossing and picking up* June's *coat*) It might have been quite innocuous. (*She follows to* R *of* June)
June. Innocuous! (*She raps the table behind the sofa*) They are trying to kill me and you call that innocuous. Somebody's leaked it to her—another Australian probably. The place is rampant

with them: they're multiplying like rabbits. (*She goes to the table* LC *and picks up her cheroot*)

ALICE. You're imagining things.

JUNE. No, no, not rabbits—opossums. Those dreary little pests.

ALICE (*moving above the sofa*) Well, anyway, what did you *do*?

JUNE (*moving to the sideboard*) I left.

ALICE (*moving to* L *of the sofa; alarmed*) You walked out of the rehearsal? (*She removes her rubber gloves*)

JUNE (*subdued*) I wasn't going to let some illiterate bitch wink at me. (*She picks up a bottle of gin and a glass and takes them to the table* LC)

ALICE (*biting her lip*) They won't like it. (*She crosses to the arch* R)

JUNE. I've given six years devoted service to this programme.

ALICE. You said yourself: they don't like contract artists to have tantrums.

(ALICE *exits to the hall and deposits the coat, the tea-cloth and her rubber gloves*)

JUNE (*excitedly*) They have no right to do this to me. I'm a senior member of the cast.

(ALICE *re-enters from the hall*)

If they wanted to—(*she swallows*) write me out—(*she pours a drink*) they should have asked me to come to the office in a proper manner. (*She returns the bottle of gin to the sideboard, replacing it with a bang*)

(ALICE *picks up a doll from the pouffe then sits on the pouffe and hugs the doll*)

ALICE. Nobody wants to write you out. It's unthinkable. *Applehurst* couldn't survive without you.

JUNE (*sitting* R *of the table* LC) Don't you be too sure. *Applehurst* is more than a village, you know—it's a community, it's a way of life. It doesn't depend on individuals. (*In a country accent*) There's many a stone in that churchyard . . .

ALICE. You talk as if it was real.

(JUNE *leans forward and raises her voice*)

JUNE (*in her own voice*) It is real to millions. It stands for the traditional values to English life—common sense—tenacity—our rural heritage . . .

ALICE. Oh, belt up!

JUNE. You're getting above yourself, missy.

ALICE. You *are* the serial. It would be nothing without you.

JUNE. Stranger things have happened. Only the other day Ronnie said to me: 'There'll have to be some changes, you know.'

ALICE. He probably meant the story line.

JUNE. No—no—it's the axe again. We're losing listeners, and

they're looking for a scapegoat. It's over a year since old Mrs Prescott was kicked by a horse. (*She drinks*)

ALICE. Yes, and look at the rumpus there was over that. And she was only a minor character.

JUNE. She had her following.

ALICE. She hardly had a line to say from one week to the next.

JUNE. What about the time I nursed her back to health, when she had concussion?

ALICE. That was exceptional.

JUNE. No, no, no. She had nice little bits and pieces here and there. When she found that stray dog, and the village adopted it . . . (*A dark thought occurs to her*) Until it was run over by a tractor. (*She shudders*)

ALICE. There's no comparison. Mrs Prescott . . .

JUNE (*rising and shouting*) Mrs Prescott had a following. (*She leaves her drink on the table*)

ALICE (*shrugging*) All right—Mrs Prescott had a following.

JUNE (*moving down* L) The subject is now closed.

ALICE (*after a pause*) But she *was* expendable.

JUNE (*crossing to Alice; angrily*) Are you trying to aggravate me? Are you deliberately trying to annoy me?

ALICE (*loudly*) You're the most popular character in it. (*She rises*)

JUNE. Don't screech at me. It's an ugly, grating sound.

ALICE. Well, look at your ratings.

JUNE. They are down. Four per cent last week—I'm slipping. Now do you understand? (*She moves* C)

ALICE (*after a pause*) You still get the most fan mail, don't you? (*Still holding the doll, she goes to the small table down* R *and takes a threaded needle from the work-basket*)

JUNE (*sitting* R *of the table* LC) Only just. Ginger, the publican, is close on my heels. Ever since he had that win on the Premium Bonds, and gave the money to Farmer Bromley, so that they wouldn't turn his place into a broiler house . . .

ALICE (*moving* RC) What about young Rosie?

JUNE (*conspiratorially*) Aha!

(ALICE *looks puzzled*)

She's preggers.

ALICE. No! (*She sits on the pouffe*) You mean the actress . . .?

JUNE. No, the character, blockhead! We reckon that'll bring back some listeners.

ALICE (*intrigued*) Who was responsible? (*She sews the skirt of Emmeline, the doll*)

JUNE. We haven't been told yet. I think it was Lennie, her steady. If so it'll be absolutely splendid. They can get married—everybody loves a wedding. But Arthur thinks it was Roy.

ALICE. Who's Roy?

June. That soldier—stationed at the army camp at Oakmead. He took her to that dance, remember?

Alice (*concerned*) What's she going to do—about the baby?

June. Well, she confides in me—in the next instalment. Comes to me in tears; wants to get rid of it. (*She sighs*) Don't know what the younger generation's coming to.

Alice. What do you tell her?

June. What *don't* I tell her. (*She puts out her cheroot in the ashtray on the table* LC) I give her a dressing-down she won't forget in a hurry. (*She rises, moves to* L *of Alice and speaks in her country accent*) Where is he? Mr Clever Lad? Show me where he is so's I can tear some strips off him, the fine young fellow. Just don't you aggravate yourself, my dear—leave it to me. Just you tell me who it was, my dear. Just you tell me who it was.

Alice. And does she tell you?

June. No. (*She pauses, crosses to* R *of the table* LC *and sits*) But I'll wheedle it out of her, never fear. Just give me three instalments, that's all. (*She picks up her drink*)

Alice (*tensely*) They shouldn't talk about—things like that.

June (*happier now*) It's nice, though, the way they come to me with their troubles. Oh, they know they'll get straight talking from me. (*In her country accent*) No lard ever passed my lips. No, sir, fine words butter no parsnips.

Alice. What *are* you talking about?

June (*putting down her glass and leaning forward*) They *need* me. Get that into your thick head. *Applehurst* needs a District Nurse. Who'd deliver the babies, who'd look after the old folk, I'd like to know.

Alice. Exactly. (*She finishes her sewing, rises, leaves the doll on the pouffe and crosses to June*) Nobody's suggesting . . .

June. What do you mean—nobody's suggesting? Why did that woman enquire after my health? Why did she wink at me, eh?

Alice. Perhaps she fancies you. (*She gives a slight snigger and crosses to* R)

June. This is no time for jesting.

Alice (*replacing the needle in the work-basket*) How do I know why she winked at you? Perhaps she's got a nervous twitch. (*She tidies the things in the work-basket*)

June (*picking up her glass, rising and moving down* C) She's Australian, dunce! They're extroverts, not neurotic townsfolk, like us. They come from the bloody bush.

Alice (*becoming exasperated*) Well, I don't know why she winked at you.

June. Oh, shut up! Silly bitch! (*She moves to* L *of the table behind the sofa, puts down her glass, picks up a framed certificate and reads*) 'And in recognition of your devoted work and care for the old and sick, we name the Geriatric Ward the Sister George Ward.' (*She replaces the certificate*)

(ALICE *applauds slowly and ironically*)

Take care, Childie, you're trailing your coat . . .

ALICE (*giggling*) You're the bull. (*She moves to the pouffe, kneels on it with one knee and puts the doll's clothes straight*)

JUNE (*dangerously*) We're very cocky all of a sudden.

ALICE (*mock innocently*) Who—me?

JUNE. Yes, you. (*She moves* C) And what the hell are you doing at home on a Tuesday afternoon? Why aren't you at work?

ALICE. Mr Katz gave us the day off. It's a Jewish holiday.

JUNE (*suspiciously*) Oh, really! What holiday?

ALICE. I don't know. The Feast of the Contamination, or something.

JUNE. You seem to have more holidays than work days lately.

ALICE (*picking up the doll and moving to the fireplace*) Not my fault.

JUNE (*still suspicious*) He hasn't been having another 'go' at you, your Mr Katz, has he?

ALICE (*moving to the table behind the sofa and putting the doll on it; primly*) Certainly not.

JUNE. I bet he has.

ALICE. He hasn't. I'd tell you.

JUNE. I wonder. (*Self-pityingly*) Nobody tells me anything.

ALICE. That's because you always make such a stupid fuss about things. (*She sits on the right arm of the sofa and puts her feet on the fender*)

JUNE. All right, then, I won't make a fuss. (*She moves to* L *of the sofa*) Come on, tell me.

ALICE. There's nothing to tell.

JUNE (*venomously*) You expect me to believe that after what happened last time?

ALICE. Nothing happened.

JUNE. A four-inch tear and three buttons off your blouse and you call that nothing.

ALICE (*angrily*) I told you. I got it caught in the Gestetner.

JUNE. Don't lie to me, Childie.

ALICE (*rising and moving above the sofa*) I'm not lying. (*She crosses towards the kitchen door*)

(JUNE *intercepts* ALICE, *grasps her arm and turns her to face her*)

JUNE. Then why are you avoiding my eyes?

ALICE. Because—because . . . Oh! (*She throws off June's hand*) You're impossible, George.

(ALICE *runs up the two steps and exits up* L *to the bathroom*)

JUNE (*calling*) Don't throw tantrums with me, young lady. (*She leans over the banister and roars*) Come out! Come out this instant.

ALICE (*off* L; *calling*) I shan't.

(JUNE *turns, picks up Emmeline the doll from the table behind the sofa, moves up* LC *and calls towards the bathroom*)

JUNE. Can you hear me, Childie? I've got Emmeline here, your favourite doll. (*Softly but clearly*) And if you don't come out of the bathroom *at once*—I'm going to pull Emmeline's head off.

(ALICE, *tear-stained, rushes in up* L, *tears the doll out of June's hand and hugs it*)

ALICE. Monster! (*She moves down* C)
JUNE (*moving to* L *of Alice*) There, that's better. (*She pauses*) And now: apologize.
ALICE. What for?
JUNE. For causing me unnecessary aggravation.
ALICE. I'm sorry.
JUNE (*crossing to* R *of Alice*) You don't sound it.
ALICE. Look, George, I know that you're worried and every-thing, but that's no reason . . .
JUNE. Don't answer back. Don't be cheeky.
ALICE. Look, George . . .
JUNE. Has Mr Katz 'had a go' at you?
ALICE (*screaming*) No!
JUNE. Don't screech at me. Apologize this instant, or there'll be severe chastisement.
ALICE. I'm sorry.
JUNE. That's better. Now, down on your knees.
ALICE. Must I?
JUNE. Yes. Come on.

(ALICE, *still hugging the doll, goes on her knees*)

Show your contrition.
ALICE. How?
JUNE. You must eat the butt of my cigar.
ALICE. I couldn't; it would make me sick.
JUNE (*standing over Alice*) Are you arguing with me?
ALICE. O.K. Hand it over.

(JUNE *crosses to the table* LC. *picks up the ashtray and holds it out to* ALICE, *who takes the cigar butt. This is actually a piece of chocolate previously concealed in the ashtray*)

JUNE. Good girl. Now eat it.
ALICE. Can I take the ash off?
JUNE. You may take the ash off, but you must eat the paper.

(ALICE, *with an expression of extreme distaste, eats the butt*)

ALICE. Ooh, it tastes vile.
JUNE. Good.

(*The telephone rings*)

That'll teach you to be rude.

(ALICE *jumps to her feet, rushes to the telephone, lifts the receiver, sits on the sofa at the right end of it, with her feet up and speaks with her mouth full*)

ALICE (*into the telephone*) Hello . . . Miss June Buckridge? . . . One moment, please.

JUNE (*moving above the sofa; apprehensively*) Who is it?

ALICE. Don't know.

JUNE (*moving to R of the sofa*) Why didn't you ask, fathead? (*She takes the receiver from Alice. Into the telephone*) Hello, this is June Buckridge. Who wants her? . . . Yes, of course . . . Yes, I'll hold on . . . (*She puts her hand over the mouthpiece. To Alice*) God Almighty, Childie, it's the B.B.C.

ALICE (*trembling*) Oh, Lord, I hope it's nothing serious.

JUNE (*into the telephone*) Hello? . . . Hello, Mrs Mercy, dear . . . No, of *course* not . . . Quite . . . Quite . . . Yes, I—there was something I wanted to talk to you about . . . Perhaps we'd better have a man-to-man . . . You have something to say to *me*? . . . No, I'm not doing anything at the moment . . . Well, I'd rather not come back to Broadcasting House today . . . Yes, yes, that's a *splendid* idea. *Love* to see you . . . That's right: Devonshire Street —top floor. You press the bell, and one of those 'I speak your weight' machines answers . . . (*With a rather forced laugh*) Yes, you know the kind of thing . . (*She intones in a deep voice*) 'You are thirteen stone two.' . . . No, no, of course not—I wasn't implying that you were . . . Yes, that'll be absolutely lovely . . . *Any* time . . . 'Bye. (*She replaces the receiver and wipes her brow*) She's coming round. She'll be here in a minute. Oh, God, I'm for it. (*She crosses to L of the sofa*)

ALICE (*putting the doll on the table behind the sofa*) Who was it?

(JUNE *goes to the table* LC, *takes a cigar from the box and lights it with the lighter*)

JUNE. The Assistant Head—Mrs Mercy Croft.

ALICE. The one who has that weekly spot on *Woman's Hour*?

JUNE. 'Ask Mrs Mercy.' Yes, that's her.

ALICE (*rising*) But she sounds awfully nice on the radio—at least her advice is sort of—sensible.

JUNE (*pacing nervously down* L) She *is* nice. (*She tries to convince herself*) Mrs Mercy is a *nice woman.*

ALICE (*crossing to* LC) Well, then.

JUNE (*crossing below Alice to the fireplace*) She's coming to see me, you understand? First she asked to see me in her office, now she's asking to see me.

ALICE (*after a pause*) Did she seem friendly?

JUNE (*tensely*) Yep.

ALICE. It'll be a good thing to clear the air.

JUNE (*moving to* R *of Alice*) You don't know what you're talking about. She wants to see me on an urgent matter. We must brace ourselves for the worst.

ALICE. Will she expect some tea?

JUNE. Tea, oh, God, yes! (*She turns Alice round and gives her a push towards the sideboard*) You must make her something special—at the double.

(ALICE *clears everything from the table* LC *on to the sideboard*)

ALICE. There's that piece of Dundee cake that mother sent. (*She takes a lace tablecloth from the sideboard cupboard and spreads it on the table* LC)

JUNE (*pacing* R) That'll be absolutely first class. (*She paces to* LC) And make her some of those Scotch scones of yours. And when you're serving the stuff, try to make a good impression, look cheerful, keep your shoulders back. And if she speaks to you don't open your mouth about things you don't understand.

ALICE. I can quite easily go out. (*She gets three teaspoons and three knives from the sideboard drawer and puts them on the table, then takes three cups, saucers and small plates from the sideboard cupboard and puts them on the table*)

JUNE. What, and leave me to pour out and all that pansy stuff. Not likely. (*She crosses to the fireplace*) You'll stay here and do some work.

ALICE (*setting out the china, etc.*) Look, George, try not to show her how worried you are. You always get sort of—aggressive when you're nervous.

JUNE (*moving* C) Go on. Back to the kitchen where you belong. (*She roughly tidies the cushions on the sofa*)

ALICE. I wish you'd do relaxing exercises or something.

(ALICE *exits to the kitchen*)

JUNE (*shouting after Alice*) I'll do relaxing exercises on your behind in a minute. (*She collects her brief-case and puts it on the floor* R *of the radiogram*) Now then. (*She picks up two framed certificates from the top of the radiogram and reads*) 'Personality of the Year.' I'll put that in a prominent position. (*She puts the certificate on the mantelpiece and reads the second certificate*) 'The English Village Preservation Society.' (*She puts the certificate on the right end of the table behind the sofa, then goes to the radiogram and moves a third framed certificate into a better position*) 'The Variety Club of Great Britain.' (*She moves a silver cup along the top of the radiogram*) 'The Association of British Nursing Sisters.' (*She moves another cup along and then picks up a silver statuette, faces front, holds out the statuette and reads its inscription*) 'Miss Humanity'—(*she pauses*) 'nominated by the Daily Mirror.' (*She places the statuette on the left end of the table behind the sofa and turns to the radiogram*) There's something missing. (*She calls*) Alice.

ALICE (*off; calling*) I'm busy.
JUNE (*moving down* C; *imperiously*) Come here. I want you.

(ALICE *enters from the kitchen, carrying a washing-up mop*)

ALICE. What is it *now*? You're always interrupting.
JUNE (*pointing to the trophies*) There's one missing.
ALICE. I haven't touched anything.
JUNE (*moving to* R *of the table* LC) There's one missing, isn't there?
Go on—have a look. I want to hear you tell me, in your own words,
which one is missing.
ALICE (*without looking*) I don't know.
JUNE (*softly, but with deadly emphasis*) Where is the Honorary
'Stag'?
ALICE (*uncertainly*) What . . .?
JUNE (*in the same tone*) What have you done with it?

(ALICE *is silent*)

I'll give you ten seconds to confess. (*She waits, breathing heavily*)
ALICE. Let me get on with the tea. She'll be here in a minute.
JUNE. You've destroyed it, haven't you? (*She pauses*) Where is
the Honorary 'Stag'?
ALICE (*after a pause*) I threw it away.
JUNE (*moving to Alice*) You—what?
ALICE (*slightly hysterically*) I *hated* it. A cut-off stag's head, im-
paled on a pike. You had no right to keep such abominations in
the house—you know I like animals.
JUNE. When did you—throw it away?
ALICE (*looking at June*) Last night.

(*There is a pause.* JUNE *sits* R *of the table* LC, ALICE *sits* L *of it*)

JUNE. You know it meant a lot to me—to be nominated
Honorary 'Stag'.
ALICE (*very contrite*) I'll get it back; I'll get another.
JUNE (*tragically*) Too late.
ALICE. I'll phone up the Town Hall—the Borough Litter Dis-
posal Unit . . .
JUNE (*tragically*) You mean the dustman, don't you? Why can't
you bloody well say so?

(*There is a long ring from the front door buzzer*)

It's her. (*She stubs out her cigar on a tea plate*)

(ALICE *rises*)

(*She rises and crosses to the speaker* R) It's the bitch, the cow, the
plague spot, the embossed carbuncle. (*She pulls out the extending
arm of the speaker and speaks into it*) Hello, Mrs Mercy, dear . . .
Yes, we're expecting you . . . Top floor. (*She pushes the speaker back
against the wall and crosses to* C) Don't stand there, gawping. Blow

your nose. Pull your sweater straight: you look disgusting. (*She tweaks Alice's sweater down like an angry mother*) Now, remember: be polite and keep mum. (*She moves* R) I'll speak to you later. (*She pauses*) Where the hell has she got to?

ALICE. Maybe she got stuck in the lift.

JUNE (*aghast*) Oh, my God, I forgot to close the lift gates.

ALICE (*moving* R *of the table* LC) I'll do it.

JUNE (*in a hoarse whisper*) Don't—it's too late.

(*The front door bell rings*)

She'll either walk, or . . .

ALICE (*suddenly scared*) Let's not open the door.

(JUNE *throws Alice a glance expressing contempt and strides out through the arch* R)

JUNE (*off* R) Oh, hello, Mrs Mercy.

(*The front door is heard to close*)

I'm so sorry—I forgot to tell you that the lift was out of order.

(MRS MERCY CROFT *enters through the arch* R. *She is a well-groomed lady of indeterminate age, gracious of manner and freezingly polite. She is wearing a navy blue two-piece suit, matching hat and accessories, and a discreet double string of pearls round her neck. She carries a brief-case*)

MERCY (*as she enters; cheerfully*) Not at all—I never use the lift. (*She sees Alice*) Oh? (*She moves* C)

(JUNE *enters through the arch*)

JUNE (*moving* RC) This is Miss Alice McNaught—Mrs Mercy Croft.

MERCY (*smiling but not shaking hands*) How do you do? (*She turns to June*) Yes, I always say: we get far too little exercise these days. If we walked upstairs instead of using lifts, those extra inches would disappear.

ALICE (*the mop behind her back; trying to be helpful*) I sometimes walk . . .

MERCY. *You* don't need to lose any weight, my dear.

JUNE (*at Alice*) Alice was just preparing the tea.

MERCY. Oh, that *is* nice. (*She smiles politely at Alice*)

(JUNE, *while* MERCY *is looking away, makes a furious gesture to Alice to go into the kitchen*)

I do hope I haven't put you to any trouble—inviting myself out of the blue.

JUNE } (*together*) {Rubbish!
ALICE }   {Not at all.

(ALICE *exits to the kitchen*)

MERCY. May I look round? (*She moves up* C) I *adore* looking at other people's flats—they do reflect their occupiers' personalities in an uncannily accurate way.

(JUNE *moves to the fireplace*)

(*She looks around*) To be perfectly honest, I imagined your home to be—different.

JUNE. Really?

MERCY (*indicating the ornaments on the bookcase*) This charming Victoriana—the dolls—somehow . . .

JUNE (*slightly embarrassed*) They're Miss McNaught's.

MERCY. Oh, of course, that would explain it. They just weren't *you*. I didn't know . . .

JUNE (*rather sheepishly*) Yes, I have a flat-mate.

MERCY (*sympathetically*) How nice. It's so important to have—companionship—especially when one's an artist.

JUNE (*moving down* R *and indicating the brasses on the wall*) These are mine—I collect horse brasses.

MERCY. How useful. (*She moves to the window*) May I look out from your window?

(JUNE *moves up* R *of the sofa*)

I love overlooking things. I've always adored heights. In my young days, my husband and I often used to go mountaineering —in the Austrian Alps for preference. (*She looks out of the window and gives a sudden yell of delight*) Ah! There's B.H.! You can see Broadcasting House from your window—isn't that—*super*! To have that reassuring presence brooding over you, seeing that you don't get into mischief.

(JUNE *laughs nervously.*
ALICE *raises the hatch* L *and leans through*)

ALICE. Ready in a minute.

MERCY. Oh—good.

JUNE. Kindly close that hatch.

(ALICE *withdraws and slams the hatch down*)

Sometimes I have the insuperable desire to decapitate her. (*She laughs*)

MERCY (*moving to* L *of the sofa*) Oh, poor Miss McNaught. I do like your settee cover—a homely pattern. I love a floral design—I know it's old-fashioned, but . . .

JUNE. Childie—Miss McNaught—made them.

MERCY (*putting her brief-case, handbag and gloves on the table behind the sofa*) Really. How clever of her—they're beautifully fitted. You're fortunate to have such a handy companion.

JUNE (*moving down* R; *in her country accent*) Yes, she's good with the needle, I'll say that for her.

MERCY (*lightly*) That was Sister George speaking.

JUNE (*in her own voice; self-consciously*) One can't help slipping.

MERCY (*moving below the sofa*) But you *are* Sister George far more than Miss June Buckridge to all of us at B.H.

JUNE. Jolly nice of you to say so. (*She indicates to Mercy to sit on the sofa*)

(MERCY *sits on the sofa, at the left end of it.* JUNE *sits in the armchair* R, *with her knees apart*)

MERCY. Thank you. You have made the part completely your own. It was obvious—even at the first auditions. I remember it quite clearly, although it must be—oh . . .

JUNE. Almost six years ago. I was scared stiff.

MERCY. How charming! One can't imagine you scared stiff.

JUNE. I don't mind actual physical danger. You know, I almost like it. I was in the A.T.S. during the war.

MERCY. Lovely!

JUNE. None of that sissy ENSA stuff for yours truly.

MERCY. It wasn't that bad.

(*There is a slight pause.* JUNE'S *smile fades*)

As a matter of fact, I did a bit of organizing for ENSA myself.

JUNE. I'm sorry. No offence meant.

MERCY. None taken. (*She reaches over the back of the sofa and gets her brief-case*) Now, Miss Buckridge—or may I call you Sister George, like everybody else?

JUNE. Certainly.

MERCY. As you know, I hold a monthly 'surgery' in my office, when I welcome people to come to me with their problems. I've always made it a rule to be approachable. But in certain cases, involving matters of special importance, I prefer to visit the subjects in their own homes, so that we can talk more easily, without any duress. That's why I'm here today.

JUNE (*in her country accent*) Ah, well, a farmer's footsteps are the best manure. (*She laughs*)

MERCY. Quite. But there is rather a serious matter I wish to discuss with you.

JUNE. I see.

(ALICE *enters from the kitchen, carrying a tray of tea. She has removed her apron*)

ALICE. Sorry I took so long. (*She puts the tray on the table* LC)

MERCY (*slightly annoyed at the interruption, but politely*) Ah, lovely! (*She rises. To* June) We'll continue our little chat after tea.

ALICE. If you'd rather . . .

JUNE (*rising and moving* RC) You can speak quite freely, Mrs Mercy. Miss McNaught and I have no secrets from each other.

MERCY. Oh. Well, let's all have tea first.

(ALICE *moves the chair* L *of the table* LC *and places it above the table*)

(*She moves above the table* LC) I say, what delicious-looking scones.

(ALICE *moves the chair down* L *and places it* L *of the table*)

ALICE. They're Scotch scones. (*She goes to the hatch, opens it and collects a plate with a lump of Dundee cake with four small slices of cake arranged beside it. She leaves the hatch open and puts the plate on the table* LC)

JUNE. They're Childie's speciality. Copied from a recipe of her grandmother's. (*She sits* R *of the table*)

(MERCY *sits above the table, and* ALICE *sits* L *of it*)

MERCY. They look delish! May I try one?

ALICE. Help yourself. (*She puts the plate of scones in front of Mercy*) Here's the jam. (*She passes the jam-pot to Mercy*)

MERCY (*taking a scone and spreading it with jam*) They're what we used to call 'Girdle Scones'.

JUNE (*mocking Mercy's inflection*) Or 'Drop Scones'.

ALICE. It's frightfully important not to get the girdle too hot, or the outside of the scones will brown before the inside is cooked.

MERCY. They're a lovely even colour.

(ALICE *pours tea for Mercy and herself but not for June*)

ALICE (*very animated*) I always cool them in a towel.

MERCY. Do you?

ALICE. Yes, and I wait till the bubbles rise to the surface before I turn them over.

MERCY. They're very successful.

ALICE. I use half a level teaspoon of bicarbonate of soda——

MERCY. Now you're giving away trade secrets.

ALICE. —and one level teaspoonful of cream of tartar——

JUNE. Shut up!

(*There is a moment's silence*)

ALICE. —eight ounces of flour——

JUNE (*exploding*) Shut up!

ALICE (*softly but firmly*) —and one egg.

JUNE. Shut up! (*She picks up the lump of Dundee cake and hurls it at Alice*)

(ALICE *ducks. The cake flies to pieces against the sideboard. There is a pause during which* MERCY *continues to eat unperturbed*)

MERCY. Now then, girls!

ALICE (*after a pause*) She hates me to talk about food. (*Confidentially*) She's a wee bit overwrought.

JUNE (*rising*) Overwrought my arse! (*She stumps over to the fireplace, takes a cheroot from the box on the mantelpiece, and lights it*)

ALICE (*chiding*) Now that wasn't nice—that was not a nice thing to say.

MERCY (*smiling indulgently*) I expect she picked it up in the army.

ALICE. She swears like a trooper.

MERCY. But she has a heart of gold.

ALICE. Once, she got into such a temper, that I wrote a poem about it.

JUNE (*moving below the sofa; bitterly*) Yes, she fancies herself as a poetess. Goes to the City Lit. every Wednesday night, to learn about metre and things.

MERCY. What a nice hobby.

JUNE. As a poetess, she makes a very good cook.

MERCY. It's still a question of mixing the right ingredients to make a tasty whole.

ALICE. That night she came back in a raging temper——

JUNE (*moving c*) Thank you very much, we've all stopped listening.

ALICE (*ignoring June*) —I wrote this poem. It began:

> 'Fierce as the wind
> Blows the rampaging termagant . . .'

(JUNE *prowls furiously* RC)

MERCY. Very expressive. (*To June*) And how did you like being compared to the wind?

(JUNE *blows a raspberry. There is a pause.* MERCY *drinks her tea*)

ALICE (*passing the plate of cake*) Slice of cake, Mrs Mercy?

(JUNE *sits* R *of the table*)

MERCY (*taking a slice of cake*) Just a teeny one. I mustn't be greedy. (*She spreads the cake with jam*)

(ALICE *takes a piece of cake*)

JUNE. Her mother made it. (*She continues smoking and uses her plate as an ashtray*)

MERCY. You can always tell if it's home-baked; it tastes quite different.

JUNE (*laughing*) You'd be amazed if you knew what old Mother McNaught put into it.

MERCY. I'm not even going to ask.

JUNE. I'm delighted to hear it. (*She laughs*)

MERCY (*enjoying herself*) Oh, dear, this is just like a dormitory feast—all this girlish banter. (*To June*) I bet you were a terror at school. (*She eats her cake*)

JUNE. I was captain of the hockey team and a keen disciplinarian—God help the girl I caught—(*in her country accent*) making me an apple-pie bed. (*She chuckles*)

MERCY. Ah, there's Sister George again. It's wonderful how over the years the character's *evolved.*

ALICE. Who first thought of putting her on a Moped?

JUNE. That was because of the sound effects. As long as I was on the old bike, listeners never knew whether I was static or mobile.

MERCY. It's a unique sound—Sister George on her Moped, whizzing through the countryside, singing snatches of hymns. (*She drinks her tea*)

JUNE. I got into a terrible row the other day because I sang a hymn which sounded like '*On the good ship Venus . . .*'

MERCY. A traditional air?

JUNE. I've found it safer to stick to hymns. Once I tried a pop song, and d'you know—hundreds of letters came in protesting.

MERCY. We learn from experience. But we don't want *Applehurst* falling behind the times.

JUNE. No. (*She looks away. Worried*) No, of course not.

MERCY. But we must constantly examine criticism, and if it's constructive, we must act on it. Ruthlessly.

JUNE. What sort of criticism?

MERCY. Oh, nothing in *particular.* At least . . .

JUNE. But *what?*

MERCY. Well, that, I'm afraid, brings me—(*she rises*) to the unpleasant part of my business.

ALICE. Oh, dear!

MERCY. But first, would you show me to the little girls' room?

JUNE (*rising*) Alice—show Mrs Mercy to the . . .

ALICE (*rising and moving up* L) This way, Mrs Mercy.

> (ALICE *exits up* L.
> MERCY *follows her off*)

JUNE (*muttering*) 'Little girls' . . .' (*She moves to the table behind the sofa, stubs out her cigar in the ashtray on it, and looks off up* L)

ALICE (*off*) It's that door there.

> (JUNE *sees Mercy's brief-case on the sofa, looks off* L, *hurriedly picks up the brief-case, crosses to the armchair* R *and opens the case.*
> ALICE *enters up* L *and stands at the top of the steps*)

(*Aghast*) What are you doing?

JUNE (*turning*) Shh! Keep a look-out. (*She rummages in the case*)

ALICE (*moving up* C) You can't, you mustn't.

JUNE (*taking a folder from the case*) My own personal file.

ALICE (*in an hysterical whisper*) Put it back!

> (JUNE *searches in the folder, takes an envelope from it and reads the inscription*)

JUNE. 'Sister George. Confidential.'

> (*The sound of a water cistern flushing is heard off* L)

ALICE. She's coming.

(JUNE *quickly replaces the folder in the brief-case, moves up* R *of the sofa, closes the brief-case and puts it on the sofa. She realizes too late that she has still got the envelope in her hand, so quickly hides it behind a cushion at the right end of the sofa. She then picks up the doll Emmeline from the table behind the sofa*)

JUNE. So Emmeline said: 'I don't want any drop scones today, thank you very much.'

(MERCY *enters up* L *and crosses below the sofa.* JUNE *and* ALICE *stand rigid with suspense*)

MERCY. I got on the scales, to see if I've put on any weight. (*She picks up her brief-case*)

JUNE (*indicating the tea table*) I don't suppose . . . (*Meaning 'you would like any more tea?'*)

MERCY (*sitting on the sofa*) Now, then . . .

ALICE. I'll make myself scarce.

(ALICE *exits to the kitchen*)

MERCY. Please sit down.

(JUNE *sits in the armchair* R)

You won't hold it against me if I speak quite plainly?

JUNE. Please do.

MERCY. It's my unpleasant duty to haul you over the coals, and administer a severe reprimand.

JUNE (*with no apology in her tone*) Oh?

MERCY. Believe me, Sister George, I'd much rather let bygones be bygones . . .

JUNE (*in her country accent*) Let sleeping dogs lie.

MERCY. Precisely. But I must remind you of the little chat we had just about a year ago, after that unfortunate incident in the Club—involving a lady colleague of mine.

JUNE (*in her country accent*) Well, we don't want to rake over old embers.

MERCY. I don't intend to. But in the light of recent events, it's difficult to forget an incident as vivid as the pouring of a glass of beer over the Assistant Head of Talks. I had hoped one black mark—(*she opens her brief-case*) would have been enough for you, but this morning—(*she takes out a clip-board and removes a sheet of paper from it*) I received this memo from the Director of Religious Broadcasting. (*She hands the paper to June*) I should like to have your comments. (*She puts the brief-case beside her on the sofa, but holds the clip-board on her knee*)

(JUNE *reads the paper then jumps up violently*)

JUNE (*excitedly*) It's a lie! It's an utter, bloody lie!

MERCY (*firmly*) Please calm yourself, Miss Buckridge. Kindly hand me back the paper.

JUNE (*handing the paper to Mercy*) It's—preposterous! (*She moves up* R *of the sofa*)

MERCY (*looking at the paper as she replaces it on the clip-board*) I take it you don't deny that you were drinking in *The Bells* on the night of the nineteenth?

JUNE (*turning at the fireplace*) How the hell should I know? (*She crosses to* C *and calls*) Alice! Come here.

(ALICE *enters from the kitchen, wide-eyed and worried*)

ALICE. You want me?

JUNE. Where was I on the night of the nineteenth?

MERCY. I'm sorry to involve you in this, Miss McNaught. (*She rises*)

ALICE (*quietly*) That was a Wednesday: I was at the City Lit.

JUNE. You would be. (*She moves to* L *of Mercy*) All right; I possibly was drinking at *The Bells* on the night in question, having a few pints with the boys. There's no crime in that, is there?

MERCY. Miss Buckridge, according to this letter—(*she refers to the second paper on her clip-board*) from the Mother Superior of the Convent of the Sacred Heart of Jesus, you boarded a taxi which had stopped at the traffic lights at Langham Place . . .

JUNE. I thought it was empty.

MERCY (*reading*) 'A taxi bearing as passengers two novitiate nuns from Ireland who had just arrived at King's Cross Station.'

JUNE. How was I to know?

MERCY. You boarded this taxi in a state of advanced inebriation—(*she looks at June*) and—(*she consults the paper*) proceeded to assault the two nuns, subjecting them to actual physical violence.

ALICE (*moving below the table* LC) You didn't really!

JUNE. No, no, no, of course not. I'd had a few pints—I saw this cab, got in—and there were these two black things—screaming blue murder.

MERCY. Why didn't you get out again?

JUNE. Well, I'd had a very nasty shock myself. What with their screaming and flapping about—I thought they were bats, vampire bats. It was they who attacked me. I remember getting all entangled in their skirts and petticoats and things—the taxi driver had to pull me free.

MERCY. A deplorable anecdote. (*She refers to the paper*) According to the Mother Superior, one of the nuns required medical treatment for shock, and is still under sedation. (*She pauses*) She thought it was the devil. (*She moves to the sofa, sits on it at the right end and replaces the clip-board in her brief-case*)

ALICE. George, how could you!

JUNE (*moving to* R *of Alice*) Don't you start on me. Back to the kitchen. Washing up. Presto!

ALICE (*firmly*) No, I'm staying here. (*She sits* L *of the table* LC) This concerns me, too.

JUNE (*moving up* C) It was all a ghastly mistake.

MERCY. No doubt, but it'll take some explaining.

JUNE. Fancy reporting it to the Director of Religious Broadcasting. What a nasty thing to do for a holy woman. (*She moves to* L *of the sofa*)

MERCY. The Mother Superior is responsible for the nuns in her charge.

JUNE (*leaning over the left arm of the sofa to Mercy*) Then she should jolly well teach them how to behave in public. I got the fright of my life, in there. Those nuns were like *mice*—albino mice—with teeny little white faces and weeny little red eyes. And they were vicious, too. They scratched and they bit. (*She bares her arm*) Look —you can still see the tooth marks—do you see that? I've a good mind to make a counter-complaint to the Mother Superior. (*She moves up* R *of the table* LC) They deserve to be scourged in their cells.

MERCY (*wearily*) I can hardly put through a report to the Controller, informing him of your allegation that you were bitten by two nuns.

JUNE. No, well, you could say . . .

MERCY. Let's be practical, Sister George—we're concerned with retaining the trust and respect of the public. Now people are perfectly well aware that artists frequently work under great emotional stress. We do all we can to gloss over minor disciplinary offences, but we simply cannot tolerate this sort of behaviour. It's things like this which make people resent paying more for their wireless licences. Thousands of pounds spent on public relations—(*she rises and moves* RC) and you jeopardize it all with your reckless and foolish behaviour. Really, Sister George, we have every reason to be very, very angry with you.

(JUNE, *beaten, sits wearily* R *of the table* LC)

JUNE. What do you want me to *do*?

MERCY (*moving to* R *of June*) You must write a letter immediately to the Mother Superior, apologizing sincerely for your behaviour, and I suggest you offer a small donation for some charity connected with the Convent. Then you must send a copy of your letter to the Director of Religious Broadcasting, with a covering note from you, couched in suitable terms.

JUNE. You mean: humbling myself?

ALICE (*rising and moving above the table* LC) Don't worry, Mrs Mercy, I'll see she does it and I'll make quite sure she doesn't get into any mischief in the future.

MERCY. There speaks a true friend. (*To June*) You're very lucky to have someone like Miss McNaught to rely on. Treasure her. (*She crosses to* R *of the sofa, then moves above it and collects her gloves, handbag and brief-case*)

June (*bitterly*) I'll treasure her all right.

(ALICE *moves to the sofa, sits on the left arm of it and puts her feet on the seat*)

ALICE. I'll see to it that the letters are written and sent off right away.

MERCY (*moving down* RC *and putting on her gloves*) Good. That's what I like to hear. (*To June*) I'll leave you in Miss McNaught's expert charge.

JUNE. What about *Applehurst?*

MERCY (*non-committally*) That's another, rather more complex problem.

JUNE (*rising and moving to* L *of Mercy*) But—has anything been decided about the future?

MERCY. I'm afraid I can't say anything about that at the moment.

JUNE (*moving down* L) It comes as a bit of a shock to me, you know, all this.

MERCY (*moving* C) It comes as a bit of a shock to me, too, I assure you, particularly as I understand that you often open church bazaars.

(JUNE *turns slowly to face Mercy*)

ALICE (*rising and moving to* R *of Mercy*) I'll look after her. I'll keep her away from convents.

MERCY. You keep her on a tight rein, and all will be well.

ALICE. I'm sure it will. Between us we'll keep her in order.

MERCY (*jocularly*) She won't stand a chance, will she?

(ALICE *moves down* R, *and keeps a steady look on June throughout the next passage*)

JUNE (*moving to* L *of Mercy*) Look here—I'm sorry—you know— if I've been a bad boy.

(MERCY *turns her charm on* JUNE *and shakes hands with her*)

MERCY. Well, good-bye, dear Sister George. Keep your chin up. Things are never as bad as they seem.

JUNE (*in her country accent; listlessly*) Every cloud has a silver lining.

MERCY. That's the spirit. And—(*she whispers confidentially*) no more walk-outs at rehearsals, eh? If you have any complaints please come and see me about them.

JUNE (*in her country accent*) Well, it's the creaking gate that gets oiled.

MERCY (*reflecting for a moment*) A somewhat unfortunate simile.

(JUNE *looks at Mercy*)

(*She turns to Alice*) So nice to have met you.

ALICE (*moving to* R *of Mercy*) Nice to have met *you*, Mrs Mercy.

(MERCY *crosses to the arch* R)

(*She follows to* L *of Mercy*) What's the subject of your talk to-morrow? Is it a secret, or are you allowed to tell?

MERCY. It's family planning this week and foundation garments next.

(MERCY *and* ALICE *exit to the arch.* JUNE *moves* RC *and looks nervously after them*)

ALICE (*off*) Good-bye.

(*The front door is heard to close.* JUNE *turns away quickly to* LC. ALICE *enters* R *and stands in the archway* R)

(*She gives June a meaningful look*) Well!

JUNE (*alarmed*) Did she say anything? Did she drop any hints behind my back?

ALICE (*moving above the sofa; sarcastically*) No. Just general comments—you know—about—(*angrily*) nuns in taxis. (*She collects June's gin glass from the table behind the sofa*)

JUNE. What do you mean?

ALICE (*crossing to the sideboard*) Nuns. You know—N-U-N-S. Brides of Christ. (*She bangs the glass down on to the tray on the sideboard*)

JUNE (*moving* C) Oh, I see what's biting you.

ALICE (*moving above the table* LC; *in an outburst*) How could you! How could you make such an exhibition of yourself? (*She stacks the crockery on to the tray*)

JUNE (*trying to laugh Alice out of it*) Oh, come on, be your age. Don't be so bloody—*squeamish*.

ALICE (*primly*) I think you owe me some sort of explanation.

JUNE (*chuckling*) When I think of all those petticoats . . . (*She waves her arms*)

ALICE. It's the sort of thing you used to do when I first knew you. In that club in Notting Hill Gate. I remember how you used to go clomping about, without a bra, hitting girls over the head. (*She picks up the tray and puts it through the hatch*)

JUNE. Kindly keep your foul-mouthed recollections to yourself.

(ALICE *returns to the table* LC)

In my young days . . .

ALICE (*collecting the jam and plates*) Your young days were spent in a cul-de-sac in Aldershot, with the Band of Hope on one side and the Foot Clinic on the other. You told me so yourself. (*She puts the jam and plates through the hatch*)

JUNE (*angrily*) How dare you! (*She moves to the sofa and sits on it at the right end*) This is a respectable house—and I'll thank you to remember who's paying the rent.

ALICE (*folding the tablecloth*) Not much longer, perhaps.

JUNE. They wouldn't dare get rid of me because of this—of this trivial incident.

ALICE (*imitating June's country accent*) We none of us know what the future may hold for us. (*She puts the tablecloth in the sideboard cupboard*)

JUNE (*after a pause*) Childie, I'm worried. I say, do me a favour.

(ALICE *reaches through the kitchen door and collects a dust-pan and brush*)

ALICE. What? (*She goes to the sideboard and brushes up the remains of the cake thrown by June*)

JUNE. Go and ask Madame Xenia to come up. She's an expert on the future.

ALICE. Oh, I can't. She's probably got a client.

JUNE. Maybe she's between appointments. Go on.

ALICE (*kneeling and sweeping up crumbs L of the table LC*) I can't just barge in . . .

JUNE. Well, it wouldn't be the first time. Remember when I was bitten by that Lakeland Terrier and you thought I had rabies. She can always tell us what's going to happen. Go on.

ALICE (*rising; exasperated*) Ohhh! (*She returns the dust-pan and brush to the kitchen*)

JUNE (*rising and moving C*) This is an emergency. Extreme measures must be taken. Go and get her at once.

ALICE. I can't. She hates my guts.

JUNE. Madame Xenia? Why?

ALICE. She thinks I'm after her lodger.

(JUNE *looks menacing*)

It's complete fantasy.

JUNE (*in her country accent; ominously*) There's no smoke without fire.

ALICE. Just like the last one you scared off.

JUNE (*in her own voice*) I could see which way the wind was blowing. I soon nipped that in the bud.

ALICE. I only helped him with his homework. He was a mere boy.

JUNE (*decisively*) There is nothing mere about boys. Now go and fetch her at once and watch your step.

ALICE. You've always got to have someone to do your dirty work. (*She trails off and crosses to R with the slummocky walk typical of all her movements throughout the play*)

JUNE. Thanks—you're a pal.

(ALICE *exits through the arch R*)

(*She moves to L of the table behind the sofa, picks up the framed certificate and reads it*) '. . . and in recognition of your devoted work and care for the old and sick.' (*She replaces the certificate, moves to* R *of the sofa, remembers the envelope and takes it from behind the cushion. She is tempted, does not dare to open it, replaces it behind the cushion and crosses to* C)

ALICE (*off* R) I'm so sorry to drag you away.

XENIA (*off* R) That's all right. I know. I know.

(MADAME XENIA *enters through the arch* R. *She is a hawk-faced, elderly woman of foreign origin, hennaed and hung with beads. She carries a little evening bag with a pack of playing cards in it.*

ALICE *follows her on*)

George! George? Darling? What's the matter?

ALICE (*moving down* R) Madame was in the middle of a consultation with a client.

JUNE. Oh, I *am* sorry.

XENIA (*crossing to* R *of June and embracing her*) Never mind. You are my friend. (*She holds June at arm's length*) Always you come first. Now—(*she pats June's arm*) darling, what's the matter?

JUNE. Madame Xenia, I'm worried out of my wits. It's the B.B.C. They're driving me mad.

XENIA (*crossing above June to the table* LC) They will suffer for it. I will put curses on them. (*She sits above the table* LC. *To June; professionally*) Sit down; make yourself at home.

JUNE. Thanks. (*She sits* R *of the table* LC)

XENIA. Oh, I'm sorry, I forgot. I always say it to people to make them relax. Right. Would you draw the curtains, please? (*She takes the cards from her bag*)

JUNE (*rising*) Certainly. (*She goes to the window and closes the curtains*)

XENIA (*to Alice*) And you: will you please sit facing the East.

ALICE (*looking around*) Which way's the East?

XENIA (*pointing* L) There. Towards Great Portland Street. (*She shuffles the cards*)

ALICE (*sitting on the pouffe and facing* L) Yes, of course.

(JUNE *moves* C)

XENIA (*looking at June*) I require a personal possession from you——

(JUNE *looks startled*)

—to hold in my hand. To connect with your vibrations. Anything —a piece of jewellery . . .

JUNE (*sheepishly*) I don't wear jewellery. Will a hankie do? (*She takes a handkerchief from her pocket then resumes her seat* R *of the table*)

XENIA (*taking June's handkerchief*) Beautiful. Now to work. First a warning. Next week will be tough for Sagittarians—Mars is in conjunction with Venus, and I don't have to tell you what that means. (*She puts the cards on the table*) Cut the cards.

JUNE (*cutting the cards*) All right?
XENIA. Again.

(JUNE *cuts again*)

And once more, just for luck.

(JUNE *cuts again*)

ALICE. As the bishop said to the actress.

(XENIA *turns up one card from each little pile*)

JUNE (*to Alice; sternly*) We can dispense with observations from the East.
XENIA (*scrutinizing the cards*) A short journey to see a friend; a pleasant surprise; unexpected money. (*She turns up another card*) The Queen of Spades—a woman in black you do not like?
ALICE. The Mother Superior?
JUNE. Shut up!
XENIA. Whoever it is—keep out of her way—she's no good to you.
JUNE (*stuttering*) What—what is she going to do?
XENIA (*consulting the cards*) She's inviting you to a big do.
JUNE (*incredulously*) The Mother Superior?

(ALICE *giggles and* JUNE *laughs with her*)

XENIA. I see lots of people, lots of drink, dancing . . .
ALICE (*lightly*) I know! It's not the convent—it's the drag ball at Richmond.
XENIA (*continuing with the cards*) Maybe. A slight emotional upset.

(JUNE *and* XENIA *look at Alice*)

Nothing serious. (*She looks at the cards*) You hear of a broken romantic association. You catch a cold—a very bad cold.
JUNE (*alarmed*) When?
XENIA (*thoughtfully*) Maybe it's because I'm holding your handkerchief. Forget the cold. (*She returns the handkerchief to June*) What else? (*She looks at the cards*)
JUNE. My career.
XENIA. I can see a red-headed man.
JUNE (*turning to Alice*) Ginger the publican. (*To Xenia*) What's he doing?
XENIA. I'm afraid it's not very clear. Ah! I see a letter—a very important letter.
ALICE (*suddenly remembering*) The envelope!
JUNE (*panic-stricken*) The envelope.
ALICE }
JUNE } (*together*) The envelope!

(ALICE *rises and runs to the sofa.* JUNE *jumps up*)

XENIA (*helpfully*) It could be a postcard.

ALICE (*snatching the letter from behind the cushion*) Here it is. (*To June*) Do you want to open it?

JUNE (*anguished*) No.

ALICE. Let's send it back to her—tell her she must have dropped it out of her bag.

JUNE (*crossing to Alice*) No, no. It's fallen into our hands—we'd better read it.

XENIA (*rising and crossing to June*) May I see the envelope?

JUNE. Yes, of course. (*She gives the envelope to Xenia*)

(XENIA *steps mysteriously down* C *and holds the envelope to her cheek*)

Do you—do you get any—vibrations?

XENIA (*carefully*) Mmm. It's difficult to say. It could mean one of two things.

JUNE (*squaring her shoulders*) Give it to me. I'm going to open it. (*She takes the envelope from Xenia, crosses down* LC *and opens it*) What must be, must be. (*She glances at the contents and collapses on to the chair* L *of the table* LC) Oh, my God! (*She drops the letter to the floor*)

(ALICE *rushes and kneels* L *of June.* XENIA *kneels and picks up the letter*)

ALICE. George! What's the matter? George!

(JUNE *remains impassive.* XENIA *reads the letter*)

(*To Xenia*) What does it say?

XENIA (*reading*) 'Memo from Audience Research. Latest Popularity Ratings.' (*She rises slowly*) 'Sister George sixty-four point five per cent. Ginger Hopkins sixty-eight.'

(ALICE *collapses, sitting back on her heels*)

JUNE. That's the weapon they've been waiting for. (*She rises*) Now they'll kill me.

JUNE *rushes towards the bedroom door up* C *as—*

the CURTAIN *quickly falls*

ACT II

Scene i

SCENE—*The same. A week later. 4 a.m.*

Before the CURTAIN *rises, as the house-lights fade, the 'Applehurst Theme' is heard.*

When the CURTAIN *rises, the music fades. By the light of the table-lamp on the sideboard and shafts of light from the archway* R, JUNE *can be discerned sitting* R *of the table* LC, *her head in her arms. She is wearing a dressing-gown over pyjamas. On the table beside her is a bottle of gin, a tumbler, a press-cutting book and her spectacles. The window curtains are open and show a faint blue light outside. After a few moments,* JUNE *is roused from her torpor by the sound of an alarm clock in the bedroom up* LC.

JUNE (*looking up; startled*) What . . .? It must be morning. I must have dropped off. (*She calls*) Alice! Childie! Rise and shine —that's if you persist in this ridiculous enterprise. Childie!

(*The sound of the alarm ceases*)

I'm in the living-room. (*She drops her head on to her arms*)

(ALICE *enters quietly from the bedroom. She is dressed only in a black brassiere and pants and carries a bundle of clothing. She puts the clothes on the sofa, moves quietly and mischievously to* R *of* June, *and attacks her, pinching and punching her right arm*)

ALICE. Pinch, punch, first of the month.

(JUNE, *very startled, jumps up and clutches the back of her chair*)

JUNE. Are you out of your mind?
ALICE (*retreating* RC; *squashed*) It's the first of the month— October.
JUNE. You could have given me a heart attack.
ALICE. Sorry. (*She goes to the switch below the fireplace and switches on the table-lamp* R *and the standard lamp*)
JUNE (*collapsing on to the chair* R *of the table* LC) Gawd Almighty! What's the time?
ALICE (*glancing at the clock on the mantelpiece*) Ten to four. (*She takes her slippers from the pile of clothes, and puts them on*)
JUNE. When are you supposed to get there?
ALICE. There's no rush; the gang gets there at about five. Have you made out your list?
JUNE. No.
ALICE (*annoyed*) Well, why didn't you? You are a nuisance. Are

26

you sure you don't want me to try for *Swan Lake*? (*She takes a pullover from the sofa and puts it on*)

JUNE. Positive. I can't stand those bloody little cygnets prancing about in their tu-tus.

ALICE. All right, all right. Nobody's forcing you.

JUNE (*rising and stretching*) My sympathy's entirely with Von Rothbart. (*She moves to the sideboard*)

ALICE. I'll just try for *Giselle*, then.

JUNE. Yeah, you try. (*She takes a box of cheroots from the sideboard cupboard*) And *Petrushka*—don't forget *Petrushka*.

ALICE. You told me last night you didn't want to see *Petrushka*.

JUNE (*moving to the table* LC) Did I? Well, I changed my mind. (*She puts the box on the table*)

(ALICE, *exasperated, goes to the mantelpiece and collects a Covent Garden brochure and a pencil*)

ALICE. Oh, you are a nuisance! I'd put a tick against *Petrushka* and then I crossed it out, and now I've got to put a tick again. (*She kneels above the pouffe, puts the brochure on it and looks through it*) And now I can't find it.

JUNE (*sitting* R *of the table* LC) You're annoying me, you know. Stop getting so—so het-up about your bloody ballet. (*She pours a drink for herself*)

ALICE. It's all very well for you to talk—you'll be sitting at home. There's a big queue, and if you don't know what to ask for . . .

JUNE. You've got plenty of time to decide what to ask for. You're only queueing for queue tickets now. (*She drinks*)

ALICE. I know. But we've all got our lists (*She rises, moves to the fireplace and studies the brochure*) Anyway, there's no certainty that we get what we ask for: you only get so many for Fonteyn and Nureyev.

JUNE. In that case, why make a list?

ALICE (*on the brink of hysteria*) You've got to ask for it first, even if you don't get it.

JUNE. You'll get something you're *not* asking for in a minute.

ALICE (*turning to the mantelpiece and writing on the brochure*) Anyway, it wouldn't have hurt you to come with me. You're up.

JUNE. I wouldn't be seen dead with that mob. What a collection!

(ALICE *puts the brochure and pencil on the mantelpiece and crosses to June*)

ALICE. There's nothing wrong with them. They're very nice, the regulars. I've known some of them for fifteen years. Do you know—there's a woman there who follows Anya Linden everywhere.

JUNE. *Everywhere?*

ALICE (*crossing to the hatch*) Oh, shut up!

JUNE. Anyway, I did come with you one day—remember?
Never again. All that gossip and name-dropping . . .

(ALICE *reaches through the hatch and switches on the electric kettle,
then puts a spoonful of instant coffee from a tin into a mug standing
on the hatch shelf*)

ALICE. The only reason you didn't like it was because you were
embarrassed by the lorry-driver. (*She picks up a knapsack from the
floor* L *and puts it on the table* LC)
JUNE. What lorry-driver?
ALICE. The one that called at you 'That's a nice pair of head-
lamps'.
JUNE. I had totally forgotten. Besides, he was paying me a com-
pliment—unlike the gentleman in Soho, who suggested that you
should wear a pair of sun-glasses for a brassiere.
ALICE (*taking a packet of potato crisps from the hatch shelf*) Don't be
disgusting!
JUNE (*jeering*) You're my flat mate in more senses than one.
(*She pours herself a gin*)

(*There is a pause.* ALICE *puts the crisps in the knapsack*)

ALICE. George, don't drink any more.
JUNE (*dangerously*) Mind your own business.
ALICE. Night after night I find you sitting up—with a bottle of
gin and that old press-cutting book. And then you wonder why
you're tired.
JUNE. I can't sleep.
ALICE. You don't even try. (*She picks up the knapsack and crosses
to the sofa*) You must try to relax—unwind.
JUNE (*imitating; caustically*) Relax—unwind! It's easy for you to
talk.

(ALICE *puts her office skirt and slip into the knapsack*)

ALICE. You've been impossible ever since that day Mrs Mercy
came to tea.
JUNE. Well, I'm more impossible since I ran into her again
yesterday.
ALICE. Where? (*She drops the knapsack to the floor*)
JUNE. At B.H.
ALICE. Was she friendly? (*She sits on the sofa*)
JUNE. She smiled at me—with the same expression as my old
cat Tiddles had when she used to look in the goldfish bowl. Until
one Sunday my parents and I came home from church, and there
on the table lay the five goldfish—(*she demonstrates on the table*) all
neatly laid out, like sardines.
ALICE. Did she—say anything to you?
JUNE (*rising*) I'll show you what she did. Get up. Go on, stand
up. I'll show you what she did. (*She moves* RC)

(ALICE *rises and moves to* R *of June*)

You're me. I was just coming out from the studio on my way to the canteen, when I turned a corner rather sharply, and ran slap bang into her. Go on—bump into me.

ALICE (*peevishly shifting from foot to foot*) Oh, I don't want to do that.

JUNE. Don't be so soppy. *Bump into me.*

(ALICE *turns her back to the audience and feebly pushes her right shoulder against June's left shoulder*)

Oh, God help us! No, properly, daftie!

ALICE (*shifting from foot to foot*) I've got to go in a minute. (*She moves to the fireplace*)

JUNE (*moving below the table* LC) You'll wait till I've bloody well finished with you. Now then: you're coming down the corridor. (*She claps her hands and gives an imperious gesture*) Start!

(ALICE *takes a run, bumps into* JUNE *and floors her. The light increases a little for dawn effect.* JUNE *rises.* ALICE *watches with a slightly malicious smile*)

(*As Mercy*) Oh, it's you. (*She surveys Alice with Mercy's half-smile*) Chin up, Sister George. (*She pats Alice's arm and crosses below her to* R) Chin up, indeed, the lousy old cow. You noticed the way she patted my arm—as if to say 'Sorry, it can't be helped'.

ALICE. You're imagining things again.

JUNE (*moving down* R) She's been avoiding me, I tell you, and I know why.

ALICE. She was probably in a hurry to get somewhere. A committee meeting or something. (*She moves* RC)

JUNE. They've had that. And I found out what happened.

ALICE (*alarmed*) What?

JUNE (*sitting on the chair down* R) I'm to be written out of next Tuesday's episode.

ALICE. What?

JUNE. Are you deaf? I said . . .

ALICE. I heard. So what? It's happened before. Every time you go on holiday.

JUNE. But I'm not going on holiday, am I?

(ALICE *is silent*)

Sister George is confined to bed with a bad cold.

ALICE. Oh, now, that in itself . . .

(JUNE *rises, moves above the arch* R *and turns away*)

JUNE. That in itself could mean a dress rehearsal for my extinction.

ALICE (*sitting on the pouffe*) Nothing of the sort.

B

June. They want to see what it sounds like without me. If I am expendable.

Alice. What about the following episodes?

June (*grimly*) We shall know soon. The new scripts are due in the post this morning. I can see what is going to happen. (*She moves down* R *and wraps her dressing-gown tightly around her*) That cold's going to get worse—I can feel it in my bones. It'll turn to bronchitis, then pneumonia, and before I know where I am I shall be out like a light. (*She sits in the chair down* R)

Alice (*only half-convinced*) You are making a mountain out of a molehill. You've missed episodes before—it's nothing to lose sleep over.

June. That's what you think. (*She blows her nose*) Anyway, I'm not the only one.

Alice. What do you mean?

June. Did you know that you talk in your sleep?

Alice. I don't.

June. You do. I heard you. Last night and distinctly again tonight. You woke me up.

Alice (*nervously*) What did I say?

June. You were tossing about, and mumbling something. And then out it came, loud and clear.

Alice (*unconvinced*) What?

June (*leaning back with arms spread out; in a plaintive high-pitched voice*) 'Take me!'

Alice. You're lying!

June (*as before*) 'Take me, Isidore!'

Alice (*rising and moving to June*) That's a filthy lie, and you know it.

June. The 'Isidore' wasn't any too distinct: it might have been some other name.

Alice (*moving* c) I don't believe a word of this.

June (*more in sorrow than in anger*) You're having an affaire with someone, aren't you?

Alice (*looking back over her left shoulder*) I wish I were.

June (*after a pause; crushed*) That was very—unkind.

Alice. Well, you asked for it. Always nagging me. Even if I did shout 'Take me' in my sleep—and I am not aware of it . . .

June. You couldn't be, of course, because you were asleep at the time.

Alice (*moving above the table* LC) All right: even if I did, it might have meant 'take me for a walk'—or—(*brightly*) 'take me to the ballet'.

June. A likely story.

(Alice *goes to the hatch, switches off the kettle then pours hot water on to the coffee in the mug*)

Alice. You always put the nastiest interpretation on things.

June (*rising and moving* RC) In nine cases out of ten I'm right. Are you making yourself some breakfast before you go? (*She moves* C)

Alice. Just a cup of coffee. I usually have a hot pie later on with the gang. In one of the workmen's cafés. (*She picks up her coffee and sits* L *of the table* LC) It's ever such fun, really. You get the ballet crowd and the night shift from the market all mixing together.

June. Sounds scintillating.

Alice. It's ever so lively.

(June *sits* R *of the table* LC)

Why don't you get dressed and come? They'd be thrilled to see you, and everyone would ask you for your autograph.

June (*in a high-pitched tone*) 'Take me!'

Alice. Oh, George!

June. No, you run along and enjoy yourself. Leave me here—waiting for the new scripts to arrive.

Alice. I don't know what's the matter with you just lately. You've become really—morbid. You used to be such fun.

June. What are you talking about? We're going to that fancy dress ball tonight, aren't we? I bet it'll be you who'll be pale and wan tonight—after getting up at this unearthly hour.

Alice (*rising and moving to the sideboard*) I'm glad you said that. I must take my iron pills. (*She collects a small bottle of pills from the sideboard*) They help to keep me awake. (*She shakes out a pill, swallows it and replaces the cap on the bottle*)

June. Let me see them.

Alice. What for?

June (*emphatically*) Let me see them.

Alice (*handing the bottle to* June) All right. (*She sits* L *of the table* LC)

June (*examining the bottle*) Why doesn't it say what they are?

(Alice *looks nonplussed*)

There's no name on the label.

Alice. I don't know.

June (*scrutinizing the label*) All it says—(*she has difficulty in deciphering the writing*) is—'One to be taken every day, as prescribed.' (*She sniffs the bottle*) I don't believe these are iron pills at all. They're those birth pills. (*She bangs the bottle down on to the table*)

Alice. Oh, really! (*She picks up the bottle*) Dr Kunjaghari gave them to me. Why don't you go and ask him?

June (*viciously*) Because I don't trust Dr Kunjaghari, that's why. He's a quack. He's like those Indians who come to the door in turbans, flogging brass bangles for rheumatism.

Alice. Perhaps you'd like to have them chemically analysed?

JUNE. It would shake you if I did, wouldn't it?

ALICE (*rising and putting the pills on the sideboard*) You can do what you like—you'd only make yourself look ridiculous. (*She crosses to the sofa and sorts through the pile of clothing. Contemptuously*) Like that time you rang up at the office, pretending to be Mrs Katz.

JUNE. Well, it served its purpose—it gave him a fright.

ALICE. It very nearly got me the sack. He knew it was you.

JUNE. He couldn't prove it.

ALICE. He's a solicitor—he could prove anything. Can't find my socks. (*She picks up the knapsack, puts it on the armchair* R *and rummages inside*)

JUNE. I say—(*she looks benignly at Alice*) seeing you in black pants reminds me of the A.T.S. We had to wear regulation black woollen pants. We used to refer to them as our black-outs. One day, a chap came to talk to us on the subject 'What not to do with our black-outs down'. He couldn't understand why we kept giggling.

ALICE (*bringing out a pair of long white socks*) Found them. (*She sits on the pouffe, kicks off her slippers and puts on the socks*)

JUNE (*after a pause*) Your legs are unusually white—luminous white. Loooo-minous white. I don't think I've ever seen such white legs.

ALICE. They don't get much sun on them.

JUNE. There's something uniquely touching about white legs—especially when they are loo-minous white. You're pale altogether, you know. You're anaemic—you ought to take iron pills.

(ALICE *throws June a meaningful glance and puts on her slippers*)

I mean proper pills—not that muck. (*She pours herself another gin*)

ALICE. Haven't you had enough? (*She rises, crosses to the sofa, kicks off her slippers and picks up her slacks from the pile of clothing*)

JUNE (*quickly*) No. (*She raises her glass and chuckles*) To absent friends. Your health, albino mice.

ALICE (*putting on her slacks; with a smile*) You *are* naughty.

JUNE. Say that again.

ALICE. What?

JUNE (*pouring another drink*) What you just said.

ALICE. You *are* naughty?

JUNE. That's it. The same inflection. Takes me back years.

ALICE. Oh. You mean . . .

JUNE. When we first met—in Mrs Goodbody's tastefully furnished bedsitters. D'you know for weeks I watched you come and go—and never said a word to you.

ALICE (*collecting a windcheater from the sofa and putting it on*) You were different then—you hadn't become famous.

JUNE. Every morning I used to watch you go to work. Punctually at ten past nine every morning. You were always in a rush.

ALICE (*fastening the windcheater*) I had to get on the underground at twenty past.

JUNE. Often you were in such a hurry you would fall over the doorstep; or, if it had been raining, you'd come slithering out, shouting 'oops!'

(ALICE *picks up her shoes, scarf and woollen cap and puts the scarf and cap in the knapsack*)

ALICE. I had no idea you were watching me. (*She sits in the armchair* R)

JUNE. One night, I went into the bathroom just after you'd had a bath. The mirror was all steamed up, and the bath mat was moist and glistening where you'd stood on it. There was a smell of talcum powder and bath crystals—it was like an enchanted wood. I stood quite still on that mat—in your footsteps—and I saw that you'd left your comb behind. It was a small pink plastic comb, and it had your hairs in it. I kept that comb as a souvenir. And all this time I'd never spoken a word to you.

ALICE (*after a pause*) You soon made up for it. (*She puts on her shoes*)

JUNE. That night your boy friend saw you home, I knew I'd have to strike quickly.

(ALICE *rises, picks up the knapsack, puts it on the pouffe, then kneels on the floor above the pouffe*)

ALICE. That was Roger. He wanted to marry me.

JUNE (*bitterly*) That's what they all said—and you fell for it, silly goose.

ALICE (*pulling out the cap and scarf and putting them on the floor* L *of the pouffe*) Some of them meant it; Roger meant it.

JUNE. What are you talking about; Roger was already married.

ALICE (*adamantly*) He still meant it. I liked Roger; he had a ginger moustache.

JUNE. What a lot of rubbish. His moustache was ginger because he used to singe it with his cigarettes—you told me so yourself. You said that every time he kissed you it tasted all burnt and beery. (*She drinks*)

ALICE (*after a pause*) I might have had babies.

(*There is a long pause*)

JUNE (*quietly*) You haven't been lonely, exactly.

(ALICE *picks up the cap, rises, goes to the fireplace, looks in the mirror and puts the cap on. It is a babyish knitted cap which fastens under her chin*)

ALICE (*changing the subject*) There's a performance of *Petrushka* on the nineteenth. I might try for that.

JUNE (*rising; suddenly*) Shh! Shh! (*She pauses and listens*) Was that the post?

ALICE. At this time in the morning? It won't be here for hours yet. You really ought to go to bed.

(*There is a pause*)

JUNE (*crossing below the table* LC *to* L *of it; seriously*) What am I going to do? They're driving me round the bend.

ALICE. You're driving yourself round the bend. (*She crosses to* C) Why don't you go to bed?

JUNE (*sitting* L *of the table* LC; *desperately*) Because I *can't sleep*.

ALICE (*moving above the table* LC) Shall I get you some hot milk?

JUNE. Urghh!

ALICE. You'll catch cold, you know, sitting up like this.

JUNE. I've already got a cold.

ALICE (*moving above June to* L *of her*) Well, keep your throat covered up, then. (*She arranges June's collar*) Put your dressing-gown on properly. It's time we got you a new dressing-gown—this collar is all frayed. I'll put some new braid on it tomorrow. There, better?

JUNE. Thanks.

ALICE (*moving above the table* LC *and indicating the gin bottle*) Shall I put this away?

JUNE (*picking up the bottle*) No, I just want to hold it for a moment. (*She hugs the bottle*)

ALICE (*moving* C *and looking at the clock*) I ought to be going—it's half past four. (*She turns to June. Worried*) Will you be all right? (*She moves to* R *of the table* LC *and faces June across it*)

JUNE. Childie, they won't do it, will they? They *can't*, after all I've done for them.

ALICE. Of *course* they won't, George. You must stop brooding about it. You'll make yourself ill. (*She sits* R *of the table* LC) Why don't you go to bed and try and sleep it off? You can set the alarm to wake you for rehearsal tomorrow.

JUNE. There's no rehearsal tomorrow.

ALICE. That's good, then. You can get a nice long rest. (*She pauses a moment, then rises and moves* R) Now George, I've got to go.

JUNE (*looking yearningly across at Alice*) No, wait a minute.

ALICE. Oh, George, they'll be waiting for me. (*She picks up the knapsack and puts it on*) I'll be at the back of the queue.

JUNE (*rising and moving* C) You can't go like *that*, you know.

ALICE. Like what?

JUNE (*pointing to the knapsack*) You're not going on a hike, you know. Mind you, donkeys are best for loading.

ALICE. There's only a change of clothing in it, to take to the office. And a few provisions. (*She backs towards the arch* R *and puts on her scarf*) Please, may I go now?

JUNE. Did you speak?

ALICE. Yes, I said 'May I go now?'

JUNE (*considering the request*) Not before you have made your obeisances to me in the proper manner.

ALICE (*alarmed*) What do you mean?

(JUNE *breathes heavily and alcoholically for a few moments*)

JUNE. You must kiss the hem of my garment. (*With an imperious gesture*) On your knees. Go on! Down, boy, down! (*She snaps her fingers and motions Alice down stage*)

(ALICE *removes her knapsack and shrugs*)

ALICE. Oh, all right. (*She goes on her knees down* R *of the pouffe*)

JUNE (*moving to* L *of Alice*) Now repeat after me: 'I hereby solemnly swear——'

ALICE (*mechanically*) 'I hereby solemnly swear——'

JUNE. '—that I will not allow——'

ALICE. '—that I will not allow——'

JUNE. '—anyone whooomsoever——'

ALICE. '—anyone—(*she imitates June*) whoomsoever——'

JUNE. '—including Mr Katz, gratification of his fleshly instincts with me today or at any other time.'

ALICE (*quickly*) All right, all right, I swear. (*She kisses the hem of June's dressing-gown*)

JUNE (*making sweeping gestures over Alice's head*) Mind you remember, or may the curse of Satan fall on your head.

ALICE (*rising and quickly reiterating*) That's one *Giselle*, one *Petrushka*, and no *Lac*—right?

JUNE (*with enormous effort*) Rien de 'Lac de Cygnes'. C'est juste. (*She holds on to Alice's scarf. With maudlin affection*) Mon petit chou.

ALICE. All right, all right, George, let go. Let go.

JUNE (*still with affection*) What's this? (*She looks at the scarf*)

ALICE. What?

JUNE. This isn't yours, is it? (*She jerks the scarf away from Alice and looks suspiciously at it*) Where did you get it?

ALICE. Oh, come on now, give it back to me.

JUNE (*moving* C *and looking at the label on the scarf*) Who is J. V. S. Partridge?

ALICE. A young Liberal. Satisfied? (*She makes a grab for the scarf*)

(JUNE *jerks the scarf out of Alice's reach*)

JUNE. Far, far from satisfied. How long have you been entangled with this—youth?

ALICE. He's not a youth. He's forty-six.

JUNE. Bit long in the tooth for a young Liberal, isn't he? (*Fiercely*) Who is he?

ALICE (*shifting from foot to foot*) The chap from downstairs, daftie. Madame Xenia's lodger. (*She crosses behind June to* L *of her and makes a grab for the scarf*)

June (*jerking the scarf out of Alice's reach*) Ah—I thought there was some monkey business going on there.

Alice. There is not. I've only ever seen him twice.

June. How did you get his scarf, then?

Alice (*after a pause; sheepishly*) I pinched it off the hall-stand.

June. D'you expect me to believe that?

Alice (*shaken, but sincerely*) Look, George, I've never even spoken to him. It's nothing.

June. That's what you said when you went off with that estate agent for a weekend in Birmingham.

Alice (*moving L*) That was five years ago.

June. It happened once—it can happen again.

Alice (*looking away*) Nothing happened.

June (*suspiciously*) Oh?

Alice (*rounding on June; almost screaming*) Nothing!

June. Well, *nothing's* going to happen now because I forbid you to speak to him.

Alice. You must be raving mad. He's a neighbour, there's no harm in being friendly.

June (*shouting*) I forbid you to speak to him, do you hear?

Alice. I'll flipping well speak to him if I want to—why shouldn't I?

June (*venomously*) You fancy him, don't you? (*She shouts*) Don't you?

Alice. He seems perfectly agreeable.

(June's *face is contorted with suspicion*)

Yes, I do fancy him—he's a dish.

(June *steps threateningly towards Alice*)

(*She shrinks back against the sideboard*) Don't you touch me—you've no right to . . .

June. I've got every right.

Alice. I'm not married to you, you know.

(*There is a long pause then* June *hands the scarf to Alice and moves up* C)

(*In a low voice*) I'm sorry, George, but you asked for it.

June. You'd better get along, you'll be late. (*She moves* C)

(Alice *crosses to* R, *picks up the knapsack, but does not put it on*)

Alice. Look after yourself. Don't forget the party tonight.

(Alice *makes a kissing motion to* June, *but* June *has turned away and does not see it.*

Alice *exits through the arch* R. June *wanders up* C, *turns and surveys the room for a few moments, swaying slightly. She moves to the chair* R *of the table* LC *with her arms out*)

June (*in her country accent*) Ah, there's my beautiful bike. (*She pats the back of the chair*) 'Morning, old friend. We'll have you started up in no time. (*She turns the chair and places it c with the back to the audience, stands l of it, looks after Alice for a moment, then makes a starting movement with her foot, and a purring noise to indicate the start of the engine*) Prrrrm! Prrrrrrrrrrrr! (*She sits astride the chair and grasps the back as handlebars*) Prrrr! Prrrr! 'Bye, Jean, 'bye, Rosie. Tell your dad to mind his gammy leg. (*She sways the chair from side to side*) Prrrr! Prrrrr! Prrrrr! (*She sings*) 'Oh God, our help in ages past——' Prrr—prrr—prrr—'our hope for years to come.' Prrr—prrr! 'Morning, Ginger, 'morning, Vicar, my word you're up early. Prrr—prrr! Yes, first call old Mrs Hinch. Prrrr—prrrr! (*She sings*) 'Be Thou our guard while troubles last——' Prrrr—prrrr! 'And our eternal——'—prrr—'home . . .'

The Curtain *quickly falls*

SCENE 2

Scene—*The same. Late afternoon of the same day.*

Before the Curtain *rises, as the house-lights fade, the 'Applehurst Theme' is heard.*

When the Curtain *rises, the music fades. The chairs have been replaced. The hatch is cleared and closed. Through the window can be seen the pink rays of sunset, which spill into the room. It is late afternoon and becomes darker as the scene progresses. The room is empty. Laughter and shrieks can be heard off in the bedroom.*

June (*off; imperiously*) Pull yourself together. Try again, and this time do it properly.

Alice (*off*) I can't promise I'll get it right.

(*There is more laughter, then the well-known signature tune of Laurel and Hardy is heard, laboriously played on the penny whistle.*
 June *enters from the bedroom, in the costume of Hardy, and carrying a carpet bag.*
 Alice *follows* June *on, dressed as Laurel and playing the whistle. They march on in step to the tune, down the steps from the rostrum and across down* R. June *halts abruptly, which makes* Alice *bump into her.* Alice *blows the whistle in* June's *ear.* June *drops the bag on to her toe and nurses her foot*)

June (*imitating Hardy*) And what, may I ask, is the meaning of that? (*She strikes Alice's upstage arm with her bowler hat*)

Alice (*as Laurel*) Nothing, Olly. I was just playing—a tune.

June. May I suggest that you stop playing—a tune—and get on with the next bit. A-one, a-two . . .

(ALICE *and* JUNE, *side by side, do a soft-shoe dance routine, dancing across and down* L)

BOTH (*singing*) 'By the light—dum da dum da dum da dum— of the silvery moon—dum da dum——' (*They reverse and dance to* RC) 'I used to—rum dum da dum da dum da dum—with my honey and—la da da. By the light . . .'

(JUNE *turns to* L *to reverse again.* ALICE *bumps into her*)

JUNE. What was the meaning of that?
ALICE (*imitating Laurel and starting to cry*) Nothing, Olly, I was only—practising.
JUNE (*turning away and fluttering her tie*) Oh, fiddlesticks! (*She moves* R *and bends to pick up the bag*)
ALICE (*following June*) Did you say 'fiddlesticks'? (*She jabs the whistle into June's behind*)
JUNE (*straightening up and forgetting her impersonation*) Ouch, that hurt! (*She rubs her behind*)
ALICE (*moving* C; *giggling*) Sorry, Olly.

(JUNE *follows Alice and gives her a great swipe with the bowler hat on her upstage arm*)

(*As herself*) That hurt!
JUNE. Sorry, Stan.
ALICE. That's not in it.

(JUNE, *in the best Hardy manner, dusts her hands and crosses above Alice to* L *of her*)

JUNE. Let that be a lesson to you. (*She turns away down* L, *beaming*)
ALICE (*singing the Laurel and Hardy tune*) Boop-a-doo, boop-a-doo . . . (*She follows June and rams the whistle against her*)

(JUNE *seizes the whistle*)

No, no, be careful, it's Miss Broadbent's.
JUNE (*only half acting*) A very useful instrument. (*She hits Alice over the head with the whistle*)

(ALICE *squares up to June, making sounds of frustrated rage and boxing movements with her hands*)

ALICE. You, oh . . . (*She backs* C)
JUNE. That's not Laurel, daftie, that's the Three Stooges.
ALICE (*moving down* C, *taking off her hat and scratching her head*) Sorry, Olly. (*Brightly*) Olly.
JUNE. Yep?
ALICE. Give me your hat.
JUNE. What for, Stan?
ALICE. I just want to look at something. (*She puts her own hat on*)
JUNE (*thrusting her hat at Alice*) O.K., Stan.

(ALICE *bends over the bowler and spits into it slowly, then puts the hat on June's head again, giving it a little tap.* JUNE *makes no protest while this is going on, but watches coldly*)

(*As herself*) What was that supposed to be?

ALICE (*as herself; backing* RC) I don't know. Just an idea. Horseplay, you know. We're celebrating because you're back in the series, aren't we?

JUNE (*with an evil glint in her eye*) Just because the scriptwriters have cured my cold, there's no need to go raving bloody mad, you know.

ALICE. I thought it was funny.

JUNE. You thought it was funny?

ALICE. Yes, I thought it was funny.

JUNE. You thought it was funny. (*As Hardy*) Stan.

ALICE (*as Laurel*) Yes, Olly?

JUNE. Give me your hat.

ALICE. What for, Olly?

JUNE. I just want to look at something.

(ALICE *gives June her hat*)

(*She points up* R) Look up there, Stan.

(ALICE *obediently looks up* R. JUNE *goes to the table* LC, *squirts soda water from a syphon into Alice's hat then returns to* L *of Alice*)

ALICE (*staring upwards*) There's nothing up there, Olly.

JUNE. Try this, then, Stan. (*She empties the water over Alice as she puts the hat on Alice's head*)

ALICE (*as herself*) Oh! You fool—now you've spoilt my costume. (*She hits June*)

JUNE (*keeping Alice at arm's length*) Steady, now. Steady.

ALICE. What was the point of that? (*She hits June, feebly*)

JUNE. Just an idea. Horseplay, you know. (*She does Hardy's slightly reeling turn round towards* L *and puts the whistle on the table* LC)

ALICE (*crossing towards the arch* R *and brushing herself*) You are rotten. I'm all wet. Now I'll have to change my things.

JUNE (*moving* C) Don't be so soppy, woman. A drop of water never did anybody any harm.

ALICE. Oh, didn't it? All right. (*She takes the flowers from the vase on the table down* R *and moves menacingly towards June with the vase of water*)

JUNE (*laughing and backing to the table* LC) Don't! No! No! No!

ALICE. Take your punishment like a man.

JUNE (*shouting*) All right. (*She takes off her hat and stands like a martyr with arms outstretched and squared shoulders, eyes shut*) Go on— what are you waiting for?

(ALICE *quickly pulls out* JUNE's *trousers by the waist and makes to pour the water inside. Both burst into shrieks of laughter and struggle with the vase)*

No! No! No!

(They are helpless with laughter, then they straighten up and ALICE *returns the vase to the table down* R*)*

ALICE. Never mind.

JUNE *(gasping and putting on her hat)* You're like marshmallow.

(The door bell rings off R*)*

ALICE. It's Madame Xenia, come to fetch us. She's early. *(She picks up the carpet bag, moves up* C *and stops, hesitantly)*

JUNE. Well, don't stand and gape. Open the door.

*(*ALICE *gives the bag to* JUNE, *who turns her round and shoves her towards the arch* R, *giving her a good-humoured kick)*

ALICE *(imitating the Laurel and Hardy whistle and still giggling happily)* Doo-do-doo, doo-do-doo . . .

*(*ALICE *exits through the arch.* JUNE *puts the carpet bag on the floor* L *of the sofa)*

JUNE. I must get it right this time. *(She moves down* LC, *closes her eyes and winds her tie, twiddling it round, like Hardy, and turning from side to side)*

ALICE *(off* R*)* Oh! Oh, I'm sorry—we were expecting . . .

*(*MERCY *enters through the arch, looking back in bewilderment at Alice.*

ALICE *follows Mercy on and stands down* R*)*

MERCY *(moving* RC*)* I'm so sorry to intrude. I do hope it's not inconvenient. *(She turns and looks startled on seeing June)*

JUNE *(taken aback)* Not at all. I'm sorry, we were just . . .

MERCY. Playing charades?

ALICE. As a matter of fact we were just getting ready to go out—to a fancy dress ball.

JUNE *(overlapping)* Ball—fancy.

MERCY. Oh, I'll come back another time when it's more convenient. *(She moves* C*)* Perhaps Miss Buckridge could come to see me tomorrow morning, before the rehearsal?

JUNE. We're not in a rush. We can talk now. Would you have a drink?

MERCY. No, thank you.

*(*JUNE *takes the tray of drinks from the table* LC *and puts it on the sideboard)*

ALICE *(moving* RC; *cordially)* Won't you sit down, Mrs Mercy?

MERCY *(moving to the table* LC*)* Thank you, dear. I know it's most remiss of me, turning up unexpectedly like this. (*She sits* R *of the table*) Actually, I've come straight from a meeting—I felt I had to see you personally. (*She puts her handbag on the table and removes her gloves*)

ALICE (*anxiously*) The nuns?

MERCY. Oh, didn't the office tell you? We had a most charming communication from the Mother Superior. All is forgiven. But there's still the little matter of the charity.

JUNE. What charity?

ALICE. The donation you promised to give to the convent.

JUNE. Oh, that.

MERCY. It's only obliquely mentioned in the letter.

JUNE (*with a wry smile*) I didn't expect her to forget about it. (*To Alice*) Remind me to send her a cheque tomorrow. (*She moves to the table down* L) It'll help keep their Irish novices in hair shirts. (*She picks up a cigar box from the table*)

(ALICE *moves to the fireplace and makes a note on a notepad on the mantelpiece*)

MERCY. Very nice of you, Miss Buckridge. I'm relieved to see the matter settled.

JUNE (*moving and proffering the box to Mercy*) May I offer you a small cigar?

MERCY. Oh, no—no, thank you. I gave up smoking years ago.

JUNE. You don't mind if I smoke?

MERCY. Well . . .

ALICE (*moving* RC) You smoke far too much.

JUNE (*with a mock bow*) Thank you for your touching concern. (*She returns the box to the table down* L, *without taking a cigar, then moves below the chair* L *of the table*)

MERCY (*after a pause*) Well, now, Miss Buckridge, I'm afraid I have some bad news for you.

(*The lights dim a little for dusk effect*)

JUNE. Bad news?

MERCY. You're the first to be told. It's only just been decided; or rather, it's only just received the official stamp of approval.

ALICE (*terrified*) You can't mean . . .

JUNE. Be quiet, Childie.

MERCY. Yes. I'm sorry, Miss Buckridge: it's the end of Sister George.

(*There is a stunned pause.* JUNE *sinks into the chair* L *of the table* LC)

ALICE (*suddenly shouting*) But why? Why?

MERCY. Believe me, dear Miss Buckridge, the decision is no reflection on your ability as an actress. You created a character that has become a nation-wide favourite.

ALICE (*still incredulous*) But why kill her?

MERCY. Why do some of our nearest and dearest have to die? Because that's life.

(ALICE *moves slowly to the pouffe and sits on it, facing* L)

In *Applehurst* we try to re-create the flavour of life, as it is lived in hundreds of English villages.

ALICE. But she's the most popular character in it.

MERCY (*slightly uncomfortable*) I know. The B.B.C. took that into consideration. They felt—and I must say I concurred—that only some dramatic event, something that would get into the news headlines, could save *Applehurst*. We felt that in their grief, robbed of one of their greatest favourites, listeners would return again to *Applehurst* with a new loyalty, with a . . .

JUNE (*interrupting dully*) How?

MERCY (*quietly*) It's not for another fortnight. It's scheduled for the twelfth.

JUNE. But how?

MERCY (*smiling benignly*) It's just an ordinary morning in Applehurst. The chaffinch on Sister George's window-sill wakes her up as usual and is rewarded with its daily saucerful of crumbs.

JUNE (*under her breath, automatically, in her country accent*) Hello, dicky. (*She sits, staring downwards, very subdued*)

MERCY (*brightly*) Up the road, in the Old Mill Farm, young Jimmy Bromley, the scamp, wakes up with a cough and doesn't want to go to school. 'We'd better get Sister George in,' says his mother—and he's up in a jiffy. Meanwhile, punctual to the minute, Sister George finishes her breakfast and packs a basketful of preserves and cottage cheese for old Mrs Hinch, in bed with bronchitis. On with her bonnet and cape, and off she goes, striding purposefully through the autumn leaves—sound effects here—to the bicycle shed. The bolts are pushed back, and the door creaks open, and there stands her prized possession—the Moped.

JUNE (*in her country accent; quietly*) 'Morning, old friend.

MERCY. Whiz—pop—the engine starts—and away she goes. Pop-pop-pop-pop-pop-pop-pop-pop . . . 'Hurry up, Jimmy, you'll be late for school,' she calls out. 'Tell Mrs Pemberton to give you plenty of homework to keep you out of mischief.' 'I will,' the boy calls back—adding as she drives out of earshot—'I don't think.'

JUNE (*in her country accent*) Cheeky little beggar!

MERCY. A chorus of greetings follows her as she heads for the open country—the wind billowing in her cape—and bursts, as usual, into a snatch of her favourite hymn: 'Oh God, our help in ages past.' Honk-honk answers her hooter in a merry descant as she turns into Oakmead Road, and then—*bang!* Collision with a ten-ton truck.

JUNE (*very quietly*) Oh, my God! (*She puts her hand over her eyes for a moment*)

ALICE. Is it—is it . . .?

MERCY. Instantaneous. Never regains consciousness.

ALICE (*weeping*) You can't, you can't . . .

MERCY. It so happens that your death will coincide with Road Safety Week: a cause which we know has been close to you for many years.

JUNE (*recovering slightly*) I've never ridden carelessly. (*She rises and moves above her chair*) I protest.

MERCY (*anxious to placate her*) I know, I know. We're taking great care to establish it's the lorry-driver's fault.

JUNE (*pacing up* L *and turning; unconvinced*) But even so—a ten-ton truck . . . (*She paces down* LC)

MERCY. I'm sorry, but there it is.

JUNE (*with dignity*) I think I have a right to a say in my own mode of death.

MERCY (*kindly*) Now, do leave it to us, dear Miss Buckridge. Leave it to the B.B.C. We know best. We've had experience in these matters.

JUNE (*crossing above Mercy to* C) If I could have been killed in the course of duty—from some infection, perhaps. (*With a sudden idea*) An epidemic! That's it—I could go to nurse a patient somewhere up in the hills, someone suffering from some unspeakable disease . . .

MERCY. I'm sorry, Miss Buckridge, the scripts have been typed.

JUNE. But they could be altered.

MERCY. I'm afraid they've been officially approved.

JUNE (*moving down* R) Then I shall take this to a higher authority.

ALICE (*rising and moving to* L *of June*) Yes, don't let them treat you like this. You've still got your public behind you: they won't let them kill you off.

MERCY (*rising and facing June and Alice; annoyed*) I'm surprised at your attitude, Miss McNaught: I thought you'd be more sensible. I came here of my own volition, as a gesture of courtesy to a valued and trusted colleague.

ALICE. But—it's not fair.

JUNE. Shut up, Childie!

ALICE. I won't shut up.

MERCY. I was going to say that I'm sure the B.B.C. will want to find some other outlet for Miss Buckridge's talents.

JUNE. I'm still not satisfied about the—accident.

MERCY (*hard*) I'm afraid that decision is final.

(JUNE *subsides on to the chair down* R. *There is a pause*)

ALICE (*to June*) Do you think you ought to lie down? You look awful. (*To Mercy*) She hasn't been sleeping well lately. (*She puts an arm around June's shoulders*)

MERCY (*crossing slowly to* C) Oh, I'm sorry to hear that.

JUNE (*after a pause*) Will I be buried in the churchyard?

MERCY (*moving to the pouffe and sitting on it; cheerfully*) Oh, it'll be done in style. Don't you worry your head about that. There's some talk of a special memorial broadcast, with contributions from all sorts of famous people—but I shouldn't really be talking about that, as everything's still in the planning stage.

JUNE. Would I be in it? In the memorial broadcast, I mean?

MERCY. Naturally. There will be lots of recorded extracts of Sister George.

JUNE. No, I meant: would I be able to tell the people how the character developed?

MERCY. Oh, no! That would spoil the illusion.

JUNE. But you said the B.B.C. wanted to use me again.

MERCY. Yes, but not as Sister George.

JUNE (*on the brink of hysteria*) What's wrong with Sister George?

MERCY. Nothing, dear Miss Buckridge. She'll be dead, that's all.

(*There is a pause.* JUNE's *head droops.* ALICE *gently helps* JUNE *to her feet*)

ALICE. Come on, George, come and lie down. (*She leads June up* C) Come on—come on.

MERCY (*rising*) In due course, I hope to discuss ideas for a new series with you. We'll do something really exciting; I'm sure of it.

(JUNE *halts* C *and turns to Mercy.* ALICE *takes her arm away from June's shoulders and stands* R *of her*)

JUNE (*with dignity; quietly*) Mrs Mercy: I would like to thank you for coming here personally today to tell me of the—the decision. I don't really feel up to discussing ideas for a new series at the moment.

MERCY. Of course you don't.

JUNE. Please don't go. Childie—Miss McNaught—will make you a cup of tea, or something. I'll have to go and lie down— (*she moves above the table* LC) for a bit, I think. (*She picks up the bottle of gin from the sideboard and turns to Mercy*) I'll put this away, in the —(*she pauses*) cabinet. (*She moves towards the bedroom door*)

ALICE (*moving to* R *of the steps*) Will you be all right, George?

JUNE (*stopping and turning*) What did you say?

ALICE. I said: Will you be all right?

JUNE. You called me 'George' then, didn't you. You'll have to get out of that habit.

(JUNE *exits to the bedroom and is heard to bolt the door. There is a pause*)

MERCY (*moving* C) I really don't think I should stay any longer.

ALICE (*moving to* L *of Mercy*) Please stay, Mrs Mercy. I'd like you to.

MERCY. Well, of course—if I can be of any assistance . . .

ALICE. Just to have someone to talk to . . .

MERCY (*crossing to the armchair* R) I expect things haven't been easy for you—recently. (*She sits*)

(ALICE *crosses to* RC)

ALICE (*with an anxious look at the bedroom door; quietly*) She's been impossible. Life's been absolute hell. You've no idea.

MERCY. I thought as much.

ALICE. Night after night I found her sitting up, drinking. Said she couldn't go to sleep with worry.

MERCY. Did she keep you awake?

(ALICE *moves to the sofa, sits, takes off her bowler hat and puts it on the seat beside her*)

ALICE. Some nights she made such a din—you know, reciting and things—that the neighbours complained.

MERCY. I had no idea it was as bad as that.

ALICE. It's been—diabolical.

MERCY. I do feel sorry for you.

ALICE. When she gets anxious, or nervous, or anything, she has to take it out on somebody. Who do you think bears the brunt? Yours truly.

MERCY. I'm amazed you put up with it.

ALICE. I have no alternative.

MERCY. Oh, come, surely there must be lots of openings for a girl with your qualifications.

ALICE. I've been with George for seven years.

MERCY. Seven years—as long as that.

ALICE. Yes, she was quite unknown when we first met.

MERCY. I expect she was easier to get on with in those days.

ALICE. She was always very jealous: wouldn't let anyone come near me.

MERCY. What a shame. Particularly as it's so important for someone with literary ability to have contact with a lot of people.

ALICE. How did you know that I . . .?

MERCY. You mentioned your interest in poetry last time we met —you attend classes, I believe?

ALICE. Yes, every Wednesday.

MERCY. I'd like to read your poems, if I may.

ALICE. Would you? Would you, really? (*She rises and moves up* LC) Shall I get them now?

MERCY (*rising and moving* RC) No, we'd better not disturb Miss Buckridge now. Give me a ring at the B.B.C. and my secretary will fix an appointment.

ALICE (*moving to* L *of Mercy*) Oh, thank you. It's really awfully kind of you—to take such an interest.

MERCY. Have you ever thought of writing for the radio?

ALICE. It had occurred to me. You know: sometimes one hears such tripe, and one thinks . . . (*She hastily puts a hand over her mouth*)

MERCY (*with mock reproof*) I know what you were going to say.

ALICE. Sorry.

MERCY. Never mind. We all feel the same way at times. Anyway, I'm not responsible for *all* the programmes.

ALICE. I'm sure yours are by far the best.

MERCY (*very pleased*) Flattery.

ALICE. No, honestly. Years ago, before I knew you had anything to do with *Applehurst*, I listened to your talks on the wireless about people's problems, and honestly, they were really—understanding.

MERCY (*touched*) I'm so glad. (*She crosses below Alice to the table LC and collects her bag and gloves*) You've got a little problem on *your* hands—(*she looks towards the bedroom door*) and no mistake.

ALICE. A big problem.

MERCY. What are we going to do?

ALICE (*moving* C) Don't know.

MERCY (*after a pause; quietly sympathetic*) Is she always so—difficult?

ALICE. Difficult! She gets very violent—especially after she's had a few pints. You've no idea the things she gets up to.

MERCY (*sitting* L *of the table* LC) Really?

ALICE. Oh, yes. (*She looks round a little wildly, then runs quickly to* R *of the table* LC *and sits, facing Mercy*) Mrs Mercy: I'm scared. I'm scared of what will happen.

MERCY. Now don't be silly. Nothing will happen. You've been living through a difficult few weeks, that's all. It was the uncertainty that made her nervous. Now that she knows the worst she'll be much more bearable, you'll see.

ALICE. You don't know George. I don't know how I'm going to survive the next two weeks.

MERCY (*putting on her gloves*) I'll do what I can to help.

ALICE (*after a pause*) I hope she won't get in a rage and murder me.

MERCY (*startled*) Are you serious?

ALICE. Dead serious. When she gets into a temper, she's capable of anything.

MERCY. Has she ever—attacked you?

ALICE. Often. It happens all the time.

MERCY. But this is *outrageous*.

ALICE. She beats me, you know. She hits me with anything that comes into her hand.

MERCY (*with sudden sharpness*) But why do you put up with it?

ALICE (*after a pause*) I have nowhere else to go.

MERCY. Surely there's somewhere . . .

ALICE. I couldn't face living alone. Not any more.

Mercy (*overcome*) My poor child. This is terrible. (*She rises, glances at the bedroom door then moves above the table and leans over to Alice*) Look, if there's any more trouble—with George, I mean, don't hesitate to give me a ring. Please regard me as your friend.

Alice (*seizing Mercy's hand*) Oh, you are kind, Mrs Mercy.

Mercy. And we must find somewhere for you to go.

Alice (*gratefully*) Would you? Would you really?

Mercy (*patting Alice's hand*) Leave it to me. (*She moves to the table behind the sofa and looks around. After a pause*) How pretty this room looks in the evening sunlight. All these charming dolls. (*She picks up the doll Emmeline from the table behind the sofa*)

Alice. That one's my favourite. Her name is 'Emmeline'.

Mercy (*shaking the doll by the hand*) Hello, Emmeline.

(*There is a pause.* Alice *rises and moves up* lc)

Alice. Do you think I ought to go and see if George is all right?

Mercy (*speaking in a childish voice to the doll*) I should leave her where she is—the naughty woman.

Alice (*moving* c) I haven't even offered you a cup of tea.

Mercy. We haven't time for a cup of tea. We have to go. (*To the doll*) Good-bye, little Emmeline. (*She replaces the doll on the table then moves towards the arch* r)

Alice. I wish you could stay.

Mercy (*stopping and turning*) So do I. But I'm glad we had a chance to have a little chat. Now remember what I told you: if there's any more trouble, get straight on the telephone to me.

(Alice *picks up her bowler hat from the sofa and puts it on*)

That's the spirit.

Alice (*moving below the sofa; in a Laurel voice*) Gee, I'm frightened.

Mercy. Don't let her bully you.

Alice (*in a Laurel voice*) She's a devil when roused.

Mercy. Good-bye, dear. Must run. Have fun.

(Mercy *exits through the arch* r)

Alice (*mechanically*) Must run—have fun. (*She looks towards the bedroom, undecided, picks up the whistle from the table* lc *and goes to the bedroom door, playing the Laurel and Hardy signature tune. She calls*) George. (*She knocks on the door and tries the handle but the door is bolted. She calls*) George, are you all right? (*She taps on the door with the whistle and chants*) Geor-orge. (*She suddenly angrily kicks the door and shouts*) George! (*She pauses, then runs to the table* lc, *slams down the whistle on to the table and throws the bowler hat on to the sofa. Rapidly and intensely*) What am I going to do?

The Curtain *quickly falls*

At the end of the interval the house-lights go out, leaving the footlights lighting the CURTAIN, *and the following recording is heard on the front-of-house speakers.*

There is the sound of Sister George's Moped, a background of country noises, the twittering of birds, mooing and neighing, etc.

SISTER GEORGE (*singing*) 'Oh God, our help in ages past, our hope for years to come, our shelter from the stormy blast and our eternal home.'

(*The singing fades out. The monotonous sound is heard of the engine of a heavy lorry*)

BILL (*in a thick North Country accent*) You awake, Fred?
FRED (*grunting something unintelligible*) Oh, ay . . .
BILL. Won't do to fall asleep now. We're nearly there.
FRED (*in a thick North Country accent*) I'm not up to it any more—this all-night driving.
BILL. There's the turning coming up now—don't miss it.
SISTER GEORGE (*approaching; singing*) 'Oh God, our help in ages past . . .'

(*There is a sound of acceleration and changing of gears from the lorry*)

FRED. Let's get there fast—I'm hungry.
BILL (*shouting*) Look out.

(*There is a screeching of brakes, followed by an explosion*)

(*Near hysteria*) We hit her! Fred, we hit her!

(*The lorry cab door is heard to slam*)

FRED. It weren't my fault. I braked . . .
BILL. Is she . . .? My God, she looks bad. (*He calls*) Hey, there!

(*The sound of heavy footsteps is heard, coming nearer*)

FARMER BROMLEY (*in a country accent*) What happened?
BILL. Bike came round the corner, oh—fast.
FRED. I tried to brake. It weren't my fault.
FARMER BROMLEY (*panting*) I always did say it's a dangerous crossing. Is she—is she badly . . .? Holy Saints! It's—it's Sister George!
FRED. It *were*.

The 'Applehurst Theme' swells up and plays cheerfully.

ACT III

SCENE—*The same. Two weeks later. Morning.*

Before the CURTAIN *rises, as the house-lights fade, the 'Applehurst Theme' is heard.*

When the CURTAIN *rises, the music fades. It is a sunny October morning. There is an abundance of flowers everywhere, including a large yellow wreath on the window-seat, a bouquet on the table behind the sofa, a pink and red wreath* R *of the radiogram, and a white wreath* R *of the banisters. On the table* LC *there are piles of telegrams and a transistor tape-recorder.* XENIA, *discreetly dressed in mauve, is sitting* R *of the table* LC, *listening to Sister George's accident on the tape-recorder. As the 'Applehurst Theme' swells up and fades,* XENIA *switches off the transistor and wipes her eyes.*

XENIA (*overcome*) Oi oi oi—poor George!

(*The front door bell rings*)

(*She rises*) All right, all right, I come.

(XENIA *exits through the arch* R)

(*Off*) Yes, I will take them, but I don't know where I am going to put them.

(XENIA *re-enters through the arch, carrying a wreath, a bouquet, and a large cross of yellow roses*)

Soon we shall not be able to move. (*She puts the wreath and bouquet on the sofa, and leans the cross against the left end of the sofa*)

(*The telephone rings*)

(*She moves to the telephone and lifts the receiver*) They are mad. I told them we were not accepting any more calls. (*Into the telephone*) You are mad. I told you we were not accepting any more calls ... A message from whom? ... The girls of your Exchange? ... Yes, I will convey it ... Very nice of you ... Charming. Miss Buckridge will be very touched ... Who am I? ... Never you mind—I am her temporary secretary ... No, I have nothing to do with *Applehurst* ... No, I am not the old gypsy woman who stole a pig. You are beginning to make me very upset. I will not speak to you any more. And no more calls, if you please. (*She replaces the receiver*) Stupid nit! (*She crosses to the fireplace*)

(ALICE *enters from the bedroom, rubbing her eyes and yawning. She wears baby doll pyjamas*)

49

ALICE. What time is it?

XENIA (*with a black look*) Half past ten. (*She picks up the wreath and bouquet from the sofa*)

ALICE. Heavens—I'm going to be late for the funeral (*She nearly trips over the yellow cross leaning against the sofa*) Oh, not more flowers—I shall never find my things. (*She kneels, looks under the sofa, finds one slipper and puts it on*)

(XENIA *takes the wreath and bouquet and leans them against the upstage end of the bookcase*)

XENIA (*pointedly*) I have been working already two hours.

ALICE. Where's George?

XENIA (*crossing to* L *of the sofa*) Out—gone. I don't know where. I am very worried.

ALICE (*standing below the sofa*) Gone? When?

XENIA. Since early this morning. I came up with two wreaths and some lilies—she took one look, rushed into the lift, slammed the gate in my face and went down like a captain on a sinking ship—but not saluting—swearing.

ALICE (*sitting in the armchair* R) I hope she is not going to do something awful.

XENIA. I think she could not stand to be in the flat another moment with all this. (*She looks round at the flowers and picks up the yellow cross*) She felt claustrophobia—I must get out. (*She moves to the sideboard*) It has been terrible for her since the accident—nothing but the telephone—letters—reporters. (*She places the yellow cross against the centre of the sideboard*)

ALICE. She ought never to have listened to the accident—it was dreadful.

XENIA (*moving above the table* LC) Oi oi oi, I just listened to the tape again—that beautiful hymn—the screeching brakes—then —(*she puts her hands to her face*) crash, bang, wallop!

ALICE (*covering her ears*) Don't!

XENIA. It was like a gas-works blowing up—horrible. (*She shudders*) I cried again.

ALICE (*rising*) Ought we to ring up the police or something?

(XENIA *picks up the tape-recorder, goes up* L *and puts it down just off up* L)

XENIA. No. We must wait. And work. Everything must be right for her when she comes back.

(ALICE *goes to the sofa, puts the cushions at the left end and flops on to it, lying with her head* L)

ALICE. I feel so exhausted—I think it's the strain.

XENIA (*moving to* L *of the sofa*) Nonsense—it was the farewell party last night. You have no stamina. You are a—what you call it—a milksop. (*She moves to R of the radiogram and picks up a pink and red wreath*)

ALICE. I've probably caught a cold. George stuffed a peach Melba down the back of my dress. Really, she's getting worse and worse.

XENIA (*moving to L of the sofa and reading the card on the wreath*) Listen to this. 'Unforgotten, from the patients and staff of the Sister George Geriatrics Ward.' Beautiful! I could cry. (*She crosses to the sideboard*)

ALICE. She'll like that.

XENIA (*placing the wreath against the wall above the sideboard*) All wreaths against the wall. There. All beautifully organized.

ALICE. Honestly, Madame Xenia, you're a brick.

XENIA (*moving to L of the table LC; suspiciously*) Why do you say that?

ALICE. It's an expression: a friend, a help.

XENIA. I see. (*She makes a note in a notebook on the table LC*) But I promised George I would take charge today and I hold my promise.

ALICE (*rising and moving C*) Could I look at some of the telegrams?

XENIA. If you're very careful and don't get them mixed up. (*She points to three piles of opened telegrams*) Those are personal, those are official and those are doubtful.

ALICE. Let's look at some of the doubtfuls. (*She picks up a telegram*)

XENIA (*sitting wearily L of the table LC*) What I would like more than anything is a nice cup of tea.

ALICE (*moving C and reading the telegram*) Oh, no!

XENIA. What?

ALICE (*bitterly*) Trust her to get in on the act. (*She crumples the telegram and moves R*)

XENIA (*chiding*) You must not do this.

ALICE (*very red in the face*) How dare she send telegrams after all these years?

XENIA. From what person?

ALICE (*reading*) 'Heartfelt condolences. Love Liz.'

XENIA. Liz?

ALICE. A friend of George's. Before my time.

XENIA. Aha!

ALICE (*moving L of the sofa*) An absolute cow. Kept writing sarcastic little notes at first; things like 'hope you are divinely happy' and 'hope this finds you as it leaves me—guess how'. (*She sits on the left arm of the sofa*)

XENIA (*quietly*) What I would like more than anything is a nice cup of tea.

ALICE. Anyway, she stole a fountain pen and a camera off George.

XENIA (*clicking her teeth*) Tut-tut. (*She opens a telegram from the pile of unopened ones on the table*)

ALICE. 'Heartfelt condolences'—she's mocking her.

XENIA (*changing the subject*) Listen to this. Here is a nice one from my old friend the Baroness. (*She reads*) 'Shall be thinking of you today. Best wishes for a triumphant funeral. Love Augusta.' She specially put off her hairdresser so that she can listen to the funeral this morning. And she only met George once —at my Hallowe'en party last year.

ALICE. Which one was the Baroness?

XENIA. She came as Julius Caesar. At least that's what we *thought* she was meant to be.

(ALICE *rises, moves* R *and looks off through the arch*)

ALICE. I hope George isn't going to be late.

XENIA. I think it is a mistake for her to listen today. Psychologically it is a mistake.

ALICE (*wandering to the window*) Oh, I don't know. She can't just play a character for six years and miss her own exit.

XENIA. But it will upset her. (*She makes a note on the pad*)

(ALICE *picks up an orange, circular wreath from the window-seat and takes it down* L *of the sofa*)

ALICE. All her old friends will be there—people she's worked with for years. There'll be tributes paid. (*She sits on the left arm of the sofa*) There'll be a proper service. I mean to say: there's a right way and a wrong way of doing things. (*She stretches one bare leg through the middle of the wreath*)

XENIA (*shrugging*) I do not understand you.

ALICE. Maybe in your country, people . . .

XENIA (*flaring up*) What do you mean: in my country? We had state funerals which could have taught you something: twenty-eight horses with black plumes, ha!

ALICE (*bitchily*) Well, you had a lot of practice, didn't you? All those assassinations.

XENIA. Assassinations?

ALICE. Shooting people.

XENIA. Of course we shoot people we don't like. You send them to the House of Lords—what's the difference?

ALICE (*rising*) Anyway, if you expect the B.B.C. to lay on twenty-eight horses with black plumes, you're in for a disappointment. (*She throws the wreath upstage against the bottom of the radiogram and moves above the table* LC)

XENIA (*jumping up; furious*) Do you want me to go? (*She crosses towards the arch* R) Immediately I go downstairs.

ALICE (*moving to* L *of Xenia*) No, no.

XENIA (*stopping and turning*) You can explain my absence to George when she comes back. *If* she comes back. (*She turns to go*)

ALICE (*running to Xenia*) No! Madame Xenia, please stay—I didn't mean to be rude.

(XENIA *stops and turns*)

It's my nerves, I'm so worried about George—supposing she's really cracked up and thrown herself under a bus or something—what am I going to do?

XENIA (*after a pause*) No, it is not a bus. (*Mysteriously*) I read the cards this morning—it is something to do with the head.

ALICE (*moving down* RC) The *head!* Oh, no, I can't bear it.

(*The sound is heard of a door handle rattling off* R)

XENIA. Shhh! There's somebody at the door.

ALICE. George!

XENIA. Look cheerful—she must see happy faces.

(*The sound is heard of a door closing off* R. XENIA *moves to the fireplace*)

ALICE (*rushing towards the kitchen door* L) She'll kill me if she sees me walking about like this.

JUNE (*off* R; *shouting*) Open the windows and let the sunshine in.

(ALICE *realizes it is too late to escape, grabs the cross of yellow roses by the sideboard and tries to hide behind it, staying down* L)

XENIA (*apprehensively*) We are here, my darling.

(JUNE *sails in through the arch* R, *wearing an extravagant orange chiffon hat with her tweed suit and carrying a picnic basket*)

JUNE (*as she enters*) It's glorious out. (*She crosses to* C *and turns to Xenia*) Darling—how sweet of you to hold the fort—I do hope you weren't pestered too much.

(ALICE's *wreath rustles*)

(*She turns and sees Alice*) Oh God, down in the forest something stirred. (*She puts the basket on the table* LC)

XENIA (*moving* C) George, we were so worried—where have you been?

JUNE (*opening the basket*) Shopping. I picked up this marvellous Christmas Gift hamper packed full of goodies. And two bottles of Veuve Cliquot 'fifty-three. (*She takes two bottles from the basket and puts them on the table*)

XENIA. But—what for?

JUNE. I've decided to skip the funeral and have a celebration.

XENIA. Celebration?

JUNE. Yes, more a coming-out party, really.

XENIA. But who is coming out?

JUNE. *I* am.

XENIA (*looking at June's hat*) I see you bought something else, as well.

JUNE. Do you like it?

XENIA. It is *charming!* Where did you find it?

JUNE. That little shop on the corner. Saw it in the window and couldn't resist it.

XENIA. You were absolutely right. It does something for you.

JUNE. Do you think so?

XENIA. It makes you look so young. Like eighteen years.

(JUNE *and* XENIA *laugh happily.* ALICE *sniggers sarcastically*)

JUNE (*turning on Alice and moving below the table* LC) What are you laughing at? And why aren't you dressed yet? You look positively indecent.

ALICE (*putting the yellow cross on the floor down* L) I overslept. I had a bit of a hangover.

JUNE (*incredulously*) A hangover? After two glasses of shandy?

ALICE. I mixed it a bit.

JUNE. What with—ginger ale?

(JUNE *and* XENIA *laugh together at this.* ALICE *does not reply*)

(*She moves down* LC) Do you think it proper to entertain visitors in this—this unseemly attire?

XENIA (*placatingly*) Oh, please—please.

JUNE. Did you make Madame Xenia a cup of tea?

XENIA. It really wasn't necessary.

JUNE (*to Alice*) What's the matter with you?

ALICE. Don't know.

JUNE. You should have been out and about for the last three hours. Did you do your exercises?

ALICE (*defiantly*) No.

JUNE (*moving to* L *of Xenia*) Oh, God help us, she takes a Keep Fit course, you know: knee bends, running on the spot, bicycling on her back. To judge by her condition it's been singularly ineffective (*She moves to* R *of Alice*) I want a cup of tea *now*. And one for Madame Xenia. And get dressed. And look sharpish about it. (*She claps her hands*) Avanti!

ALICE (*after a pause; looking straight at June*) I think your hat is a mistake.

JUNE (*thundering*) What?

(ALICE *does not reply*)

This day will end in tears.

ALICE (*shouting*) They won't be my tears.

(ALICE *runs out to the kitchen*)

JUNE (*moving up* L *of the table* LC) The baggage! The little baggage.

XENIA (*moving* R *of the table* LC) She is upset.

JUNE (*rounding on Xenia*) She has no business to be upset: it's *my* funeral. (*She crosses to the sofa*)

XENIA (*putting one champagne bottle back into the basket and fastening the clasp*) She's taking it hard. Some people . . .

JUNE. Oh, some people are no good in a crisis. I've seen it over and over again during the war.

XENIA. Ah, the war. I was an air raid warden.

JUNE (*sitting on the sofa*) I was in the Army. Attached to the Commandos. It was tough, but by God it was rewarding.

XENIA (*picking up the basket and putting it on the floor above the sideboard*) It's lucky for her she wasn't old enough.

JUNE. Childie in the Army? That'd be a giggle. She'd have collapsed under the weight of her forage cap. (*She laughs*)

XENIA (*picking up the red and pink wreath*) Would you like to go through the latest tributes? (*She crosses to* L *of the sofa*)

JUNE. If it's absolutely necessary.

XENIA. Look at this—from the patients and staff of the Sister George Geriatrics Ward. In that hospital your name will never die.

JUNE (*firmly*) *Her* name.

XENIA. Her name, your name: it's the same thing.

JUNE. No, it's not. George and I have parted company. And do you know, I'm glad to be free of the silly bitch.

XENIA. What?

JUNE. Honestly.

XENIA. George, what are you saying?

JUNE. I'm saying that my name is *June*. June Buckridge. I'm endeavouring to memorize it.

XENIA (*laughing*) You are incredible! (*She replaces the wreath against the wall above the sideboard*)

(ALICE *enters from the kitchen, carrying a tray of tea for two, with the crumpled telegram on a side plate. She puts the tray on the table* LC *and takes the telegram on the plate to* JUNE. XENIA *sits* L *of the table* LC *and pours a cup of tea for herself*)

ALICE. I'm afraid one of the telegrams got crumpled up. You'd better read it.

JUNE. What telegram?

ALICE. Here. (*She holds out the plate*) Will there be any reply, Modom?

(JUNE *takes the telegram and reads it*)

JUNE. Liz—I don't believe it.

ALICE. I thought you'd be pleased. (*She moves to* R *of the table* LC)

XENIA (*attempting to mediate*) It's always nice to hear from old friends.

ALICE (*moving above the table* LC *and singing to the tune of 'Auld Lang*

Syne') La *la* la la la, la *la* la la . . . Sugar, Madame Xenia? (*She angrily pushes the sugar bowl towards Xenia*)

XENIA. No, thank you. I take it neat.

JUNE (*reminiscing*) She was a thoroughbred, you know, Liz: nervy, stringy, temperamental. I remember I used to tease her because her hair grew down her neck, like a thin mane, between her shoulder-blades.

(ALICE *bangs the plate down on the table* LC *and runs off into the bedroom, slamming the door violently behind her*)

(*She laughs*) Ho, I knew that would annoy her.

XENIA. She got out of bed with the left foot this morning.

JUNE. Her behaviour recently has left much to be desired. I may have to speak to her mother about it.

XENIA. She has her mother here?

JUNE. No, no, no. In Glasgow. Inoffensive old soul. Bakes cakes; minds her own business—but a terrific mumbler. Can't understand a word she says. (*She mumbles inaudibly in a high-pitched refined Scottish accent*) Ooo noo noo noo. You're far too decent, you're may guest, would you no' like a cup of tea and a hot pay about fave and twenty past fave. (*She laughs*)

XENIA (*laughing*) Oh, you are a scream!

JUNE (*rising and moving to* R *of the table* LC) Well, come on—let's open the champers. (*She looks at the flowers*) Then we can clear out some of the foliage.

(*The door bell rings off* R)

XENIA (*rising and crossing* R) I go. Soon we shall need a greenhouse.

JUNE. I say, thanks awfully for helping me out today, Madame Xenia.

XENIA. But you are my friend. For you I do anything.

(*The door bell rings off* R)

Perhaps this one is from Buckingham Palace.

(XENIA *laughs and exits through the arch*)

JUNE. And about time, too. They've been slacking. (*She untwists the wire of the champagne cork*)

XENIA (*off*) Oh. Did you want to see Miss Buckridge?

(MERCY *enters through the arch. She is dressed in mourning with a small black hat. She carries a sheaf of lilies.*

XENIA *follows her on. As* MERCY *reaches* C, JUNE *opens the champagne with a pop. Froth pours out.* JUNE *puts one hand over the mouth of the bottle and turns to ask for glasses*)

JUNE. Have you got . . .? (*She sees Mercy*)

MERCY. I do hope I'm not disturbing you.

JUNE (*surprised*) Mrs Mercy! No, of course not. (*She puts the bottle on the table* LC *and wipes her hand on her skirt*)

MERCY (*handing the bouquet to June*) Dear Sister George—for you —a little tribute—from all of us in Admin. at B.H.

JUNE (*nonplussed*) Oh. Thanks. Extremely decent of you. I— appreciate the thought. (*To Xenia*) Would you be an angel, Madame, and put them in water? (*She hands the bouquet in front of Mercy to Xenia*) Oh, I'm terribly sorry: do you know each other? This is Madame Xenia—Mrs Mercy Croft.

(XENIA *throws the bouquet into the armchair* R *then bears down on Mercy*)

XENIA. What? *The* Mrs Mercy? (*She embraces Mercy*)

JUNE. Of course. Didn't you know?

XENIA (*to Mercy*) But I love you, my dear. (*She holds Mercy at arm's length for a few moments then again embraces her*) I *adore* you.

MERCY (*clamped in the embrace*) Have I had the pleasure . . .?

XENIA (*releasing her*) You don't know me from Adam, my darling, but for twenty years I have listened to you—every single week.

JUNE. How nice. (*She picks up the bottle of champagne, goes to the sideboard and pours herself a glass of champagne*)

MERCY (*overlapping*) Charming!

(JUNE *drinks*)

XENIA (*quite overcome*) I am—I cannot tell you—your advice is a hundred per cent. A hundred and twenty per cent. One senses— you have a heart, you have suffered . . .

MERCY. Well, we all have our ups and downs.

XENIA. But you have had more downs than ups. (*She pauses briefly*) Am I right?

MERCY. I shouldn't like . . . (*She retreats above the sofa and puts her handbag and gloves on the table behind the sofa*)

XENIA. Of course I am. I knew at once. Ask George here. (*She moves up* C. *To June*) Am I ever wrong?

JUNE. Never. She is quite infallible. You see, Madame Xenia is a clairvoyant.

XENIA. A psychometrist.

JUNE. Oh, sorry. (*She sits* L *of the table and reads the notes on the pad*)

XENIA (*moving to* L *of Mercy*) I write a syndicated column every week: star forecasts—hack work, but what the hell, one's got to live.

MERCY (*moving* R *to avoid Xenia*) I'm afraid I don't really be-lieve in that kind of . . .

XENIA (*pointing at Mercy; quickly*) Be careful what you do on the tenth.

(MERCY *pauses* R *of the sofa*)

There's treachery around you. (*She moves to* L *of Mercy*) Don't sign any important document before full moon.

MERCY (*moving to the fireplace*) I'm obliged to you, but really . . .

XENIA (*following Mercy and pointing at her*) There's news from abroad . . .

MERCY (*crossing to* C; *to June*) I thought you'd be all alone this morning. That's why I came.

JUNE. Very kind of you.

(XENIA *crosses to* R *of Mercy and taps her on the shoulder*)

XENIA. You're inclined to suffer from digestive disorders. Don't worry, it's nothing serious.

(MERCY *turns to June*)

JUNE (*apologetically*) Madame is helping me out today.

XENIA (*tapping Mercy's shoulder*) A tall man doesn't like you. Avoid him.

MERCY. It would be somewhat difficult in my job to . . .

XENIA. An old association will be broken. Never mind: there are plenty of birds in the sky.

MERCY (*icily*) I think you mean fish in the sea.

XENIA (*to herself*) Interesting. (*She crosses to the armchair* R *and picks up the bouquet*) Must be born under Pisces. (*Cheerfully*) Oh, well, I'll get some water for the flowers.

(XENIA *exits through the arch* R)

JUNE. She's been marvellous today: done all the organizing.

MERCY. Isn't your friend—er—Miss . . .?

JUNE. Miss McNaught? She's not up yet. I'm afraid she's no good at times like these. No backbone. Ballast.

MERCY (*wandering up* C *and inspecting the flowers*) What beautiful tributes. May I read some? I *adore* inscriptions.

JUNE. There's a whole lot more in the bathroom. As soon as Childie's dressed she can take them all and dump them on the Cenotaph.

MERCY. But you can't do that. They're for *you*. (*She moves down* C. *Seriously*) Do you know the entire *Applehurst* company turned up for the recording today in black? It was quite spontaneous.

JUNE (*annoyed*) They must be bonkers. I can just see old Mrs Hinch. She must have looked like 'Keep Death Off the Roads'. (*She sees Mercy's black suit*) Oh, I do beg your pardon.

MERCY. We felt we couldn't let her go without some mark of respect. After all, she has been with us for—how long?

JUNE (*looking away; with assumed toughness*) Six perishing years.

MERCY. Oh, come now—you know you enjoyed every minute of it.

JUNE (*getting exasperated*) Yes, but it's over—I just want to forget it.

MERCY. I don't think your public will let you. (*She moves to* R *of the sofa and indicates the wreaths*) You can see how much you meant to them. (*She moves above the sofa*)

(JUNE, *trying to escape, rises, removes her hat and puts it on the table* LC)

JUNE. Actually, I was just on the point of changing.
MERCY. For the funeral?
JUNE. For the broadcast.

(XENIA *enters through the arch, brandishing a large, hideous, ornate vase which bears Mercy's flowers*)

XENIA (*crossing to* R *of the table* LC) All right?
JUNE (*sitting in the chair* L *of the table* LC) Wasn't there something a little more—conservative?
XENIA. I can put them in a milk bottle, if you like. Or perhaps you'd prefer a bottle of gin? (*She moves up* C *and puts the vase on the radio shelf. Piqued*) It is good to have one's hard work appreciated. Getting up early in the morning . . .
JUNE (*interrupting and overlapping*) Madame Xenia—I'm eternally grateful. You've been a brick.
XENIA. Yes, so I've been told before.
MERCY (*picking up a bouquet from the table behind the sofa*) What a charming message. (*She reads*)

'Ever-present, spirit-like
Harken! The familiar sound:
Sister George, astride her bike,
In the happy hunting-ground.'

(JUNE *mutters under her breath*)

XENIA (*moving down* RC) Well, happy hunting, Sister George.
JUNE. You're off, then, are you, dear?
XENIA. I'm afraid my client is waiting. The moment you need me, just stamp on the floor. (*She moves to the arch* R)
JUNE. I shall be absolutely all right. (*Suddenly*) I say.

(XENIA *stops and turns*)

If any more flowers come, shove them in the coal-shed.

(MERCY *moves to* R *of the banister and picks up a wreath*)

XENIA. Leave everything to me. I am your friend.
MERCY (*reading the label on the wreath*) 'Fare thee well. Go in peace, good woman.'
XENIA. I can take a hint.

(XENIA, *her nose in the air, strides out through the arch*)

JUNE (*blowing a kiss after Xenia*) Thank you, darling.

MERCY (*moving down* C) You do have a lot of friends, don't you?

JUNE. I hope so. I like to think . . .

MERCY (*moving to* R *of the table* LC) Loneliness is the great scourge of our time.

JUNE. Too true.

MERCY. I had visions of you, sitting by your set, alone with your grief.

JUNE. With Miss McNaught, actually, but it comes to the same thing. (*She laughs*)

MERCY. Frankly, I'm amazed you're taking it like this.

JUNE. Like what?

MERCY. So calmly. (*She sits* R *of the table* LC) Cheerfully.

JUNE. The uncertainty was the worst. Once that was over . . .

MERCY. You have a very strong character. (*She pauses*) Will you go on listening to the programme now?

JUNE. I don't know. I hadn't really thought. Probably not. I mean—it might be rather—distressing—you know, hearing all the old voices going on without me.

MERCY. Isn't that rather a selfish attitude to take?

JUNE. Selfish?

MERCY. You died to save the series—surely you'll want to take an interest in its fortunes?

JUNE. Well . . .

MERCY. I think the next few episodes will be particularly fascinating. (*She warms to the subject*) Your death means an enormous re-adjustment to the whole community. It will take them weeks, even months, to get over the shock. But eventually the gap must be filled; new leaders will arise . . .

JUNE. Leaders? What new leaders? Who?

MERCY (*confidentially*) Well, it's not really ready for release yet, but between you and me—I believe Ginger . . .

JUNE (*rising; horrified*) Ginger? (*In her country accent*) He couldn't lead a cow down Buttercup Hill, couldn't Ginger. (*She crosses above the table to* R *of Mercy*) He's weak. Weak as the rotten apples that fall off a tree.

MERCY. Ginger will be our new anti-hero.

JUNE (*turning to face Mercy*) An anti-hero in *Applehurst*?

MERCY. Contemporary appeal, Sister George. *Applehurst* is facing up to the fact that the old values have become outdated.

JUNE (*crossing to the armchair* R *and sitting*) I wonder how old Mrs Hinch is going to take that.

MERCY (*quickly*) Not very well, I'm afraid. She passes away.

JUNE (*aghast*) What?

MERCY. It's due the second week in December.

JUNE. How?

MERCY. It'll be a cold winter in Applehurst. She gets up in the middle of the night to let the cat in.

JUNE. And . . .

MERCY. Bronchitis. Gone in two days.

JUNE (*rising and crossing to Mercy; angrily*) But you can't do this—after all the care I've taken of that woman. Why, I've nursed her from gout to gastro-enteritis over the last six years.

MERCY. That's neither here nor there.

JUNE. I could have saved her—(*she moves to the fireplace*) just like old Mr Burns last winter. He's three years older, and—(*she turns to face Mercy*) look at him now, fit as a fiddle. At least he was . . .

MERCY. I'm afraid he's due for a stroke next Friday.

JUNE (*moving to R of Mercy*) But why this carnage, why all this slaughter?

MERCY (*rising and facing June*) We live in a violent world, Miss Buckridge, surrounded by death and destruction. It's the policy of the B.B.C. to face up to reality.

JUNE. Who's going to look after the—survivors?

MERCY. Nurse Lawrence.

JUNE. *What!*

MERCY. Yes, she arrives from the District Hospital tomorrow to take over from you. (*She moves down L*)

JUNE. But she's a probationer. She couldn't put a dressing on a—salad. (*She moves R*) They won't stand for that, you know.

MERCY. On the contrary, Nurse Lawrence wins the trust and affection of the village, and becomes known, rather charmingly, I think, as 'Sister Larry'.

JUNE. *Sister Larry!* You're going to make this ill-bred, un-educated little slut . . .

MERCY (*moving RC; shouting*) Contemporary appeal, Sister George. People like that *do* exist—and in positions of power and influence: flawed, credible characters like Ginger, Nurse Lawrence, Rosie . . .

JUNE (*squaring up to Mercy*) What about Rosie?

MERCY. She's pregnant.

JUNE. I know that. And as she's not married, either, that's about as flawed and credible as you can get.

MERCY. She's going to marry her boy friend—Lennie.

JUNE. Oh, good. Good. (*She moves to the armchair R*) I'm glad. I'm glad about that—glad. (*She sits*)

(*There is a pause*)

MERCY (*sitting on the sofa*) Mind you, it's not his baby.

JUNE. Eh?

MERCY. It's Roy's, from the army camp at Oakmead. She tells Lennie, makes a full confession; he forgives her, and they live happily ever after.

JUNE (*leaning over the arm of the chair*) Pardon me while I vomit.

(ALICE *enters from the bedroom. She is wearing a gaily coloured dress*)

C

ALICE (*moving* R *of the table* LC) Oh, hello.

MERCY (*cordially*) Hello, dear. I was wondering where you were.

ALICE. I didn't go to work today.

MERCY. No, of course not.

ALICE (*sweetly*) Can I make you a cup of tea, Mrs Mercy?

MERCY. I'd *adore* a cup of tea. (*She rises, goes to the table behind the sofa, takes a mirror from her handbag and looks in it*)

(ALICE *opens the hatch*)

JUNE (*bitterly*) Mrs Mercy's come over with the charming news that I'm to be replaced by Nurse Lawrence.

ALICE (*picking up the tea tray*) Nurse Lawrence—Nurse Lawrence? Do I know her?

JUNE. Don't be irritating. Of course you know her. That interfering busybody from Oakmead.

ALICE (*with indifference*) Oh, her. (*She puts the tea tray through the hatch*)

JUNE. Yes, *her.*

ALICE. Anyway, it's not really your concern any more what happens in *Applehurst.* You're out of it. (*She moves to the table* LC *and tidies the telegrams*)

JUNE (*rising and crossing to* R *of the table* LC) Can't you understand? Can't you understand anything? I built it up: I made it what it is. It's not *nice* to see one's life work ruined.

(ALICE *moves to the sideboard and tidies up*)

MERCY (*moving to the fireplace*) I have got one piece of cheering news for you, if you can bear to hear it.

JUNE. I can bear it. (*She sits* R *of the table* LC) Pour me out a glass of gin, Childie, while you're over at the sideboard.

(ALICE *pours a gin, hands it to June and stands* L *of the table with the bottle in her hand*)

(*She drinks*) You were saying, Mrs Mercy?

MERCY. It concerns your future.

JUNE (*putting down her glass, rising and crossing to Mercy*) My future, yes. You are quite right: we must talk of the future. Is there still time?

MERCY. There's still nearly an hour to go.

JUNE. Did you want to stay for the—the . . .?

MERCY. Broadcast?

JUNE. The funeral. Yes.

MERCY. No, I have to get back to B.H. We're having a little party, you know. Perhaps 'party' isn't quite the right word.

JUNE. A wake?

MERCY. I suppose one could call it that. That's why—(*she leads June down* R) I want a quick word with you, Miss Buckridge. Mrs

Coote has promised to come. You know Mrs Coote, don't you?
She's in charge of *Toddler Time*.

June. Yes, of course I know her: a charming woman.

Mercy. Well, dear, she's very anxious to have you.

June. Really?

(Mercy *moves the chair down* r *near to the pouffe and sits.* June
sits on the pouffe, facing Mercy)

Mercy. What I'm telling you now is strictly off the cuff.
Everything's still in the planning stage. I thought I'd nip over
and tell you that there's a ray of sunshine on the horizon.

June. I'm all ears.

(Alice *puts the bottle on the table, exits to the kitchen and removes
the tray from the hatch*)

Mercy (*confidentially*) Well, dear, as you probably know,
Toddler Time has been—what shall we say—a wee bit disappoint-
ing. Audience research figures—this is strictly *entre nous*, you
understand——

June. Yes, yes, of course.

Mercy. —show a slight, but perceptible slide. Mrs Coote, I
may tell you, is worried out of her mind. She hasn't slept a wink
for three weeks.

June (*looking away*) Poor love.

Mercy. The script-writers are running round in circles—one
of them's had a nervous breakdown: the one who wrote the series
about Tiddlywink, the Cockerel, which, as you know, was with-
drawn after only three instalments. Anyway, to cut a long story
short, there's been some agonizing re-appraisal over *Toddler
Time*. A completely new approach has been decided on.

June. Don't tell me—marauding gollywogs, drunk teddy bears,
and pregnant bunnies.

(Alice *enters from the kitchen with a tray of tea for one which she
puts on the table* lc)

Mercy (*smiling enigmatically*) Not quite, dear.

(Alice *sits* l *of the table* lc)

But we're preparing an absolutely super new adventure series, in
which we've all got loads of confidence, which will combine
exciting narrative with a modern outlook—and you're being
considered for the title role.

June. What's it called?

Mercy. '*The World of Clarabelle Cow.*'

(*There is a pause.* June *rises and moves* c)

June. Am I to understand that this—this character is a cow?

c*

MERCY. A very human one, I assure you: full of little foibles and prejudices.

JUNE (*slowly*) A—flawed—credible—cow?

MERCY. Credible in human terms, certainly. Otherwise the children wouldn't believe in her. Children are very discerning.

ALICE. Ought to be fun.

JUNE (*moving to* L *of the sofa*) I don't think I could have understood you correctly. I don't believe I really grasped the meaning of your words.

MERCY. I thought I made myself perfectly clear.

ALICE. Oh, don't be dense, George.

JUNE (*to Alice*) Shut up! (*She moves to* R *of the table* LC *and turns to Mercy*) Am I to take it that you have come here today—the day of the funeral of Sister George—to offer me the part of a cow?

MERCY. We must be practical, dear. None of us can afford to be out of work for too long.

JUNE. Pour me out another gin, Childie, will you?

(ALICE *refills June's glass*)

(*To Mercy*) You're not serious, are you? You're joking, aren't you?

MERCY (*rising*) We don't joke about these things at the B.B.C., Miss Buckridge.

ALICE (*rising*) It's jolly nice of Mrs Mercy to come over specially to tell you. (*She moves up* C)

MERCY (*crossing to* R *of June*) I thought it was a brilliant idea of Mrs Coote's.

JUNE (*shouting and tearing her hair*) I can't stand it! (*She crosses to the window*) I'm going mad!

(XENIA *enters through the arch* R *carrying a cross of white chrysanthemums*)

XENIA. One more for luck.

JUNE (*tonelessly*) Who from?

XENIA (*reading the inscription*) 'I never thought I'd survive you. Mrs Ethel Hinch.'

MERCY. She doesn't know yet.

JUNE (*crossing to Xenia; distracted*) She's going to die, Madame Xenia—in two months' time. They're going to murder her, too. An old lady of eighty-five, who's never done anyone the slightest harm.

(MERCY *moves below the table* LC)

XENIA. How terrible! (*She puts the cross in the chair* RC) Are you sure?

JUNE (*to Mercy; wildly*) Murderess!

(JUNE *lunges at Mercy*. ALICE *and* XENIA *move quickly to June and restrain her*. XENIA *grabs June by her right arm and shoulder and* ALICE *grabs June's left arm*)

ALICE $\Big\}$ *(together* $\Big\{$ George!
MERCY $\Big\}$ $\Big\{$ Really, Miss Buckridge. Restrain yourself.
JUNE. Is your blood lust sated? How many other victims are you going to claim?
MERCY (*shrilly*) Control yourself!
ALICE. George, you're drunk!
XENIA. My darling is upset. She's had a shock.

(JUNE *throws off the constraining arms and moves slowly to Mercy, making a great effort to control herself.* ALICE *stands* C. XENIA *is* RC. MERCY, *a little frightened, is below the table* LC)

JUNE (*after a pause*) With reference to *Toddler Time*, would you thank Mrs Coote for her kind interest——
MERCY. There's no need for you to decide today.
JUNE. —and tell her I cannot possibly accept the part in question.
MERCY. Very well. I'll tell her.

(*The buzzer* R *sounds.* XENIA *goes to the speaker, pulls it out and listens*)

ALICE (*moving to* R *of June*) Don't be silly, George. You can't afford to turn down . . .
JUNE. I'm not playing the part of a cow.
XENIA. A cow? What cow?
JUNE (*frantically*) I'm not playing the part of a cow!
MERCY. I've taken your point, Miss Buckridge.
XENIA (*turning to June*) There are two nuns, to see Sister George.
JUNE. No! *No!*

(JUNE, *groaning with dismay, rushes off up* L)

XENIA (*to Mercy*) Nuns before noon is a good omen.
MERCY (*moving* C) I'll take your word for it.
ALICE (*moving up* L) I'd better see what she's doing.

(ALICE *exits up* L)

(*Off; calling*) George: what are you doing?

(MERCY *moves up* C. *The sound of running bath water is heard off* L)

XENIA (*into the speaker*) I'm sorry, Sister George is getting ready for her funeral. (*She pushes the speaker back to the wall*)

(ALICE *enters up* L)

ALICE. She appears to be running a bath.
XENIA (*moving* RC) Shall I go and speak to her?
MERCY. She won't do anything silly, will she?
XENIA (*to Alice*) See if she's all right.

(ALICE *exits up* L)

(*She sits on the sofa*) I'm so worried.

MERCY (*moving above the sofa*) There was bound to be a re-action. (*She moves* R *of the sofa*)

ALICE (*off; calling*) George! (*She pauses*) I can't hear what you're saying. Turn the bloody taps off!

JUNE (*calling*) Leave me alone!

XENIA. Oi, oi, oi!

(*The sound of the water ceases.*
ALICE *enters up* L)

ALICE (*as she enters*) Says she wants to be left alone.

(MERCY *moves to the fireplace*)

XENIA. How did she sound?

ALICE. Like a walrus.

XENIA. Thank God she is herself again. (*She rises and moves to the arch* R) Oi, oi, what a morning!

(XENIA *exits through the arch. There is a pause.* MERCY, *at the fireplace and* ALICE *up* L, *face each other for a few moments, then* MERCY *extends her arms.* ALICE *runs into Mercy's arms, lays her head on Mercy's shoulder and bursts into tears.* MERCY *gently puts her arms around Alice*)

MERCY. My poor child. There, there.

ALICE. I can't stand it any more.

MERCY. I know, I know. You've been under a terrible strain.

ALICE (*breaking from Mercy*) You've no idea, Mrs Mercy.

MERCY. I can imagine.

ALICE. She's been *terrible!*

MERCY. Hush, dear. She'll hear you. (*She leads Alice to the sofa*)

(ALICE *sits on the sofa.* MERCY *sits* R *of Alice*)

ALICE. I was praying you'd come.

MERCY. I wasn't going to leave you alone with her today. (*She smiles*) Besides—I had promised.

ALICE. Oh, I know, but I knew how busy you were.

MERCY. First things first.

ALICE. I knew I could rely on you. I felt it the first time I met you.

MERCY. And I felt I was speaking to a proud and sensitive person, whose personality was being systematically crushed.

ALICE (*turning away*) Don't!

MERCY. And with a definite literary talent.

ALICE (*turning*) Honestly? Do you really think so?

MERCY. I'm being quite objective.

ALICE. Gosh! Wouldn't it be marvellous!

MERCY. What, dear?

ALICE. If I could do some work for you—writing, I mean.

MERCY. We shall see what transpires. I'll certainly give you all the help I can.

ALICE. Oh, you are nice.

MERCY. And the other offer still stands.

ALICE (*looking away*) Yes, well—I think I've almost definitely decided. I'm sorry to be so vague.

MERCY (*after a pause*) Not at all. (*She rises and moves up R of the sofa*)

ALICE. It's a bit of a wrench, you know. I've been working for Mr Katz for nearly four years. I'd have to give him a month's notice.

MERCY (*moving above the sofa*) There's no rush. I told you I'd keep the job open for a fortnight.

ALICE. And then there's George.

MERCY (*with a glance up L*) Yes.

ALICE. I mean: I don't know how she'd take it.

MERCY (*moving to L of the sofa*) You have told her, of course?

ALICE. God, no! She'd have murdered me.

(MERCY *crosses to the table* LC, *stands with her back to the audience and pours a cup of tea*)

MERCY. In view of what happened today, I think we were very wise.

ALICE. If she suspected I'd been to see you behind her back . . .

MERCY. There was no reason why you shouldn't. You're perfectly entitled . . .

ALICE. Oh, I *know*. But she's so possessive. I'm never allowed anywhere near the B.B.C. I'm kept a guilty secret.

MERCY. She's shackled you to her. (*She sits* R *of the table* LC) Anyway, you wouldn't be working for the B.B.C. You'd be working for me as my own private secretary, in my London flat.

ALICE (*rising and crossing to* R *of Mercy*) It sounds absolutely super. I'm sorry I'm being so slow about making up my mind.

MERCY. A thought has just occurred to me: if you're in any kind of trouble—you know, with George—you can always camp down at the flat. There's a divan . . .

ALICE. Oh, that'd be *wonderful!*

MERCY. It could serve as your temporary H.Q. It's not luxurious, mind. (*She drinks her tea*)

ALICE. Never mind that. It would be an escape—if necessary.

MERCY. That's what I thought. I only ever stay there myself if I've been kept late at a story conference, or something like that. I find it useful. I suppose it's a place for me to escape, too.

ALICE (*after a pause*) We'd be like prisoners on the run.

(*There is a pause.* MERCY *drinks then puts down her cup*)

MERCY. Do you really think you can escape?

ALICE (*after a pause*) I don't know. (*She moves up* C *and glances off* L)

MERCY. It's very difficult for you.

ALICE (*moving up* R) It's been so long, so many years. (*She picks up Emmeline from the table behind the sofa*)

MERCY. It's hard to break the routine.

ALICE. It's the little things one misses most.

MERCY (*smiling*) You could bring your dolls.

ALICE (*moving to the armchair* R *and hugging Emmeline*) I couldn't go anywhere without them. I even take them on holiday—and then I'm terrified they'll get lost or stolen. Sometimes George hides them—it's her idea of a joke.

MERCY. A very cruel joke.

(ALICE, *still holding the doll, runs to Mercy and kneels* R *of her*)

ALICE. Don't let her get at me, Mrs Mercy. Stay here—don't go away. (*She clutches Mercy's knees*)

MERCY. I can't stay here all day, dear.

ALICE. Please don't leave me. I'm terrified of what she will do.

MERCY. Calm yourself, Alice. No one's going to hurt you. Here, put your head on my shoulder.

(ALICE *lays her head on Mercy's shoulder*)

Close your eyes. Relax. My goodness, you're trembling like a leaf. (*She strokes Alice's hair*)

ALICE (*with her eyes shut*) That's nice.

MERCY. You're my little girl. You're going to be—my little girl.

(JUNE *enters up* L. *She is wearing her bath robe*)

JUNE. What a touching sight.

ALICE. George! (*Panic-stricken, she rises, runs* R *and shrinks against the armchair*)

(JUNE *crosses to Alice, snatches the doll from her and turns to Mercy*)

JUNE. I always did say she had nice hair. I always said that for her.

ALICE. George, you don't understand.

JUNE (*to the doll*) Did you hear what your mummy said, Emmeline? She said I don't understand. Did you see what your mummy was doing with that strange lady?

MERCY. She was overwrought, Miss Buckridge. (*She rises*) I tried to comfort her.

(ALICE *edges down* R)

JUNE. How absolutely sweet of you. And how well you have succeeded.

(ALICE *is trembling from head to toe*)

MERCY. I hope you don't think . . .

JUNE (*to Alice; sweetly*) Come here, I want to talk to you. Come on, I want to talk to you.

(ALICE *looks terrified*)

Don't be fright, I'm not going to hurt you.

ALICE. Why can't you tell me in front of Mrs Mercy?

JUNE (*feigning gaucheness*) Well, you know, boy's talk . . .

MERCY. Would you rather I left?

JUNE (*turning to Mercy*) Oh, no, no. Whatever could have given you that idea? (*She moves to Alice and grabs her arm*) Come here, I want to whisper to you. (*She whispers to Alice*)

ALICE (*breaking from June; shouting*) *No!*

(JUNE *grabs Alice again and whispers to her*)

No, I'm not going to do it. (*She runs down* L)

JUNE (*slapping the doll on her thigh to punctuate her line*) Yes or no, Childie? Yes or no?

ALICE (*frantically*) No, no, *no!*

MERCY (*white with indignation*) What are you asking her to do, Sister George?

JUNE. The suitable treatment. The punishment that fits the crime.

ALICE. She wants me to drink her bath water.

MERCY (*astounded*) Her bath water?

ALICE. To humiliate me.

MERCY. But this is preposterous! I've never heard of such an obscene suggestion.

JUNE (*moving to* R *of Mercy*) You're shut off from the world, Mrs Mercy. 'Ask Mrs Mercy—all your problems answered.' 'Dear Mrs Mercy, what shall I do? My flat-mate is nasty to me and wants to punish me by making me drink her bath water. By the time you reply to this—glug, glug, glug—it may be too late— glug—and I might have drowned.'

MERCY (*to Alice*) I strongly advise you to leave this house at once.

JUNE (*to Alice*) Well, you've had the benefit of Mrs Mercy's expert advice. Are you going to take it?

ALICE. I'm sorry, George, I can't stay with you any longer.

MERCY. Very sensible.

JUNE (*crossing below Mercy to* R *of Alice*) Did you hear what your mummy said, Emmeline? She said she's going to leave us. (*She raises the doll over her head as if to hit Alice*)

MERCY. I wish you wouldn't . . .

JUNE (*dangerously*) You keep out of this. This is between Alice and myself.

ALICE (*pleading*) Let me have Emmeline.

JUNE (*pointing the doll at Alice*) Glug, glug to you.

MERCY. I don't know how you can be so cruel. The poor child . . .

JUNE (*moving above the table* LC) 'The poor child'! As you're going to see quite a lot of 'the poor child' in the near future, I'd better put you in the picture about her.

ALICE. George, don't! George, please!

JUNE. 'The poor child' likes to pretend she's a baby, but have a look at her; go on, have a close look at her.

(ALICE *bursts into tears and sinks on to the chair down* L)

MERCY (*crossing quickly to Alice*) Can't you see you're upsetting the child. (*She puts her arm protectively around Alice*)

JUNE (*shouting*) The child? The child is a woman—she's thirty-four.

(ALICE *sobs loudly*)

She's old enough to have a grandchild.

MERCY. Oh, really, now you're exaggerating.

JUNE (*to Alice*) Am I? *Am I?*

ALICE (*whimpering*) Don't, George—don't.

JUNE (*moving down* C; *with disgust*) Look at you: whimpering and pleading. Have you no backbone, can't you stand up like a man?

ALICE (*sobbing*) I can't—help it.

JUNE (*imitating her savagely*) 'I can't help it.' She'll never be any different—feckless, self-indulgent. (*She throws the doll on to the sofa and moves up* C)

ALICE (*jumping up and running towards the bedroom door*) I'm going. I'm packing my bag.

(JUNE *intercepts Alice, grabs her by the arm and drags her* C)

JUNE. Come back here.

MERCY. Let her go. Let her go.

JUNE (*to Mercy*) You've got yourself a prize packet there, and no mistake.

ALICE (*screaming*) Let me go! (*She wrenches herself free and collapses on the floor down* C, *weeping*)

JUNE (*after a pause; looking down at Alice*) She had an illegitimate child when she was eighteen.

(ALICE *weakly covers her ears*)

She gave it away—to strangers. She's got a daughter of sixteen.

(ALICE *sobs*)

Do what you like—you make me sick. (*She sits* R *of the table, takes a drink of gin and remains sitting, not looking at the others, until the end of the scene*)

(*There is a pause.* ALICE *cries despairingly.* MERCY *moves to* L *of Alice and looks down at her*)

MERCY. Stop crying.

(ALICE's *sobs subside*)

Get up, quickly.

(ALICE *rises and stands* R *of Mercy, her head down*)

Go and pack. You needn't take everything now. Go along, hurry. I'll wait for you here.

(ALICE *exits to the bedroom*)

(*She turns to* June) I'm sorry, Miss Buckridge, about all this. It'll be all for the best, you'll see. I do hope you're not bearing me any grudge.

(JUNE *shakes her head*)

Oh, good, good. Sometimes it's best to make a clean break—it's painful, but that's the advice I always give in my programme. Which reminds me—(*she looks at her watch*) it's about time for the broadcast. Shall I switch it on? (*She moves to the radiogram and switches it on, then collects her handbag and gloves and puts her gloves on*) Let it give you strength, Miss Buckridge. Remember: Sister George was killed, not because she was hated, but because she was loved.

(ALICE *enters from the bedroom. She carries a mackintosh and a small suitcase*)

(*She moves to* R *of* June) If you study anthropology, you'll discover that in primitive societies it was always the best-loved member of the community who was selected as the sacrificial victim. They felt that by killing him the goodness and strength of the victim would pass into them. It was both a purge and a re-dedication. What you are about to hear is the purge and——

(*The slow tolling of a bell sounds softly from the radio*)

—re-dedication of *Applehurst*. Good-bye, Sister George. (*She crosses to the arch* R *and looks back*)

(ALICE *crosses to the sofa, picks up the doll Emmeline, moves to* R *of the sofa, hesitates and looks back at* June)

ALICE. I think she's right in what she said, George—Mrs Mercy, I mean. I love you, too, that's why I've got to leave you. You do understand, don't you? I mean . . . (*She weeps and looks almost impatiently at Mercy*) All right, Mrs Mercy, I'm coming.

(MERCY *exits through the arch* R)

Good-bye, George, and—you know—thanks for everything.

(ALICE *exits through the arch* R. JUNE, *who has not looked up, remains sitting* R *of the table. An* ANNOUNCER's *voice is heard from the radio, backed up by the tolling bell*)

ANNOUNCER (*through the radio*) *Applehurst,* a chronicle of an English village. This is a sad day for *Applehurst.* The church bell is tolling for the funeral of Sister George, the well-beloved District Nurse, whose forthright, practical no-nonsense manner had endeared her to the community, but death——

(*Very soft music, a slow and minor variation on the 'Applehurst Theme' is heard over the Announcer's voice and continues softly to the end of the scene*)

—comes to the best of us, and the picturesque village of Applehurst is today swathed in mourning.

JUNE (*a very plaintive sound*) Moo! (*Louder*) Moo! *Moo!* (*A heartrending sound*)

The music increases in volume as—

the CURTAIN *falls*

THE APPLEHURST THEME

FURNITURE AND PROPERTY LIST

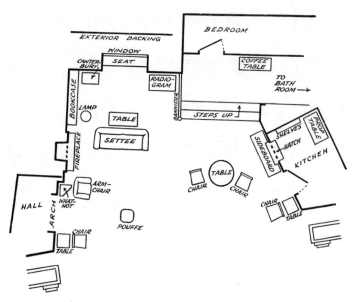

ACT I

On stage—Table (down R). *On it:* table-lamp, work-basket with threaded
        needle and other sewing things, brass vase, ash-
        tray
    Upright chair (down R)
    Whatnot (R). *On shelves:* Victorian china ornaments
    Small tub armchair (R)
    Electric fire
    Fender
    Tin waste-paper bin
    On mantelpiece: electric clock, small silver cups, ornaments, framed
       photographs, pencil, notebook, ball-point pen, small wooden box
       containing 3 cigars, small doll, table-lighter
    Long low bookcase (up R). *In it:* books
                     On it: ornaments, 2 small Victorian
                        standing dolls
    Canterbury (up R). *In it:* magazines, newspapers, 2 Victorian dolls,
                     small lamp (not practical)
    Standard lamp (up R)
    On window-seat: squab to match window curtains, small cushion,
       records in sleeves
    Window curtains
    Bureau-type radiogram. *On shelf:* radio script, spectacles
                   On top: 3 framed certificates with words
                     'Personality of the Year', 'The English

Village Preservation Society', 'The Variety Club of Great Britain'. Silver statuette of girl 'Miss Humanity, nominated by the *Daily Mirror*'. Silver cup (The Association of British Nursing Sisters)

Sofa. *On it:* cushions

Table (behind sofa). *On it:* telephone, empty cigar box, framed certificate, ashtray, salver

Pouffe. *On it:* Victorian doll 'Emmeline'.

Long coffee-table (up LC). *On it:* magazines, lamp (not practical)

Sideboard (L). *On it:* table-lamp, tray with 2 vermouth bottles, 2 sherry bottles, bottle of gin, 3 small glasses, 1 tumbler, wooden box with 2 cigars, ashtray, matches, bottle of pills

    In drawer: 3 knives, 3 teaspoons

    In cupboard: 3 cups, 3 saucers, 3 side plates, wooden box with 2 cigars, empty cigar boxes, plastic lace tablecloth

Small table (down L). *On it:* small wooden cigarette box with 2 cigars, ashtray, matches

Upright chair (down L).

Circular pedestal table (LC). *On it:* tortoiseshell box with 2 cigars, glass ashtray with chocolate, table-lighter

2 upright chairs (LC)

On wall down R: two-way speaker on an extending arm

Carpet on floor

Carpet on rostrum

Light switch below fireplace

On wall above arch: 3 miniatures

On wall below fireplace: leather strap with horse brasses

Over fireplace: oval mirror, miniatures in gold frames

On wall over bookshelves: landscape

On wall R *of window:* 3 miniatures

On wall over radiogram: trophy shield, 2 framed photographs of groups of actors rehearsing

On walls up LC: landscape, picture of ballet dancers

In hall: table. *On it:* vase of flowers
    umbrella vase

In kitchen: shelves

Window closed

Window curtains open

Bedroom door shut

Hatch closed

Kitchen door open

Light fittings off

Fire on

Off stage—Brief-case (JUNE)

    Tea-cloth (ALICE)

    Washing-up mop (ALICE)

    Brief-case. *In it:* folders with papers, envelope with memo, clipboard with papers (MERCY)

    Tray. *On it:* pot of tea, milk, sugar, plate of Scotch pancakes, jam, butter (ALICE)

    Plate with Dundee cake and knife (ALICE)

    Dust-pan and brush (ALICE)

Personal—JUNE: gloves, handkerchief

    MERCY: handbag, gloves

    XENIA: evening bag. *In it:* cards

ACT II
Scene 1

Strike—Tea things
    June's brief-case

Re-set—Chair down L
    Awards on top of radiogram

Set—*On table* LC: bottle of gin, tumbler, press-cutting book, spectacles
    On hatch: electric kettle with hot water, mug, spoon, packet of potato
      crisps, tin of instant coffee
    On sideboard: bottle of pills
    On floor below sideboard: knapsack. *In it:* Alice's white socks
    On table behind sofa: doll 'Emmeline'
    On mantelpiece: Covent Garden brochure, pencil
    On table down R: yellow chrysanthemums in brass vase
    On table down L: lighter

Window closed
Window curtains open
Bedroom door closed
Hatch open
Kitchen door closed
Fire on
Lamp L, on
Other lamps off

Off stage—Clothes (ALICE)

Personal—JUNE: handkerchief

Scene 2

Strike—Everything from table LC
    Alice's slippers
    Everything from hatch shelf

Set—*On table* LC: tray with syphon, bottle of gin and tumbler
    On sideboard: bottle of gin

Re-set—chairs to original positions

Window closed
Window curtains open
Bedroom door open
Hatch closed
Kitchen door closed
Fire on
Fittings off

Off stage—Penny whistle (ALICE)
    Carpet bag (JUNE)

ACT III

Strike—Flowers from table down R
    Whistle
    Carpet bag
    Bowler hat
    Salver from table behind sofa

Set—*Under sofa:* Alice's slipper
    On table behind sofa: bouquet of chrysanthemums, doll 'Emmeline'
    On window-seat: circular wreath of orange flowers
    R *of radiogram:* pink and red wreath

R *of banisters:* circular wreath of white roses
On table LC: transistor tape-recorder, 3 piles of opened telegrams, pile of
    unopened telegram envelopes, unopened telegram, pad, pencil
On sideboard: champagne glass, bottle of gin, tumbler
On floor below sideboard: wreath of yellow flowers
On sideboard: vase of white chrysanthemums
On coffee-table: star of yellow chrysanthemums, bouquet of tulips and other
    spring flowers, bouquet of white chrysanthemums, bouquet of Arum
    lilies
R *of bedroom door:* sheaf of lilies, bunch of snapdragons, etc., bunch of
    larkspur, etc.
L *of banisters:* bouquet of white and yellow chrysanthemums
Above radiogram: circle of red and white roses round shield on wall, bouquet
    of orange dahlias on radio shelf, bouquet of red dahlias under shelf
On window-seat: cross of pink flowers, bouquet of mixed chrysanthemums,
    bouquet of daffodils on ground
Hanging on canterbury: heart-shaped wreath of white and pink chrysan-
    themums
Hanging on standard lamp: star of pink and yellow flowers
In hearth: bouquet of white chrysanthemums, vase of yellow and white
    chrysanthemums
On top of whatnot: vase of yellow chrysanthemums, yellow star

Bedroom door shut, but unlatched
Hatch closed
Window closed
Window curtains open
Kitchen door closed
Fire on
Fittings off

Off stage—Wreath, bouquet, large cross of yellow roses (XENIA)
        Picnic basket. *In it:* tins of food, 2 bottles Veuve Cliquot (JUNE)
        Tray. *On it:* pot of tea, milk, sugar, 2 cups, 2 saucers, 2 teaspoons,
            1 side plate, crumpled telegram (ALICE)
        Sheaf of lilies (MERCY)
        Large hideous vase (XENIA)
        Tray. *On it:* pot of tea, milk, sugar, cup, saucer, teaspoon (ALICE)
        Cross of white chrysanthemums (XENIA)
        Suitcase, mackintosh (ALICE)

Personal—XENIA: handkerchief
        JUNE: orange chiffon hat
        MERCY: handbag. *In it:* mirror. Watch

LIGHTING PLOT

Property Fittings Required—electric fire, standard lamp, 4 table-lamps (2 not practical)

    Interior. A living-room. The same scene throughout

    THE APPARENT SOURCES OF LIGHT ARE—in daytime, a window up RC, and at night, a standard lamp R and table-lamps R and L

    THE MAIN ACTING AREAS ARE—R, down R, C, LC and down L

ACT I   Afternoon

To open: Effect of September afternoon sunshine
            Fire on
            Fittings off

Cue 1   JUNE closes window curtains   (page 23)
        6-second fade of upstage light leaving area pouffe—sofa—table well lit

ACT II SCENE 1 Night

To open: Room dim
            Table-lamp L, on
            Blue outside window
            Fire on
            Flood outside arch R, on

Cue 2   ALICE switches on lights   (page 26)
        Snap in table-lamp R
        Snap in standard lamp
        Snap in covering lights

ACT II SCENE 2 Late afternoon

To open: Effect of sunset
            Fittings off
            Fire on

Cue 3   After rise of CURTAIN   (page 37)
        Commence slow cross fade of lights for dusk effect

Cue 4   MERCY: '. . . news for you.'   (page 41)
        Dim lights a little for dusk effect

ACT III Morning

To open: Effect of bright sunshine
            Fittings off
            Fire on

No cues

EFFECTS PLOT

ACT I

79

Any character costumes or wigs needed in the performance of this play can be hired from Charles H. Fox Ltd, 184 High Holborn, London, W.C.1.

MADE AND PRINTED IN GREAT BRITAIN BY
LATIMER TREND AND CO. LTD, WHITSTABLE
MADE IN ENGLAND